# THE
# SECOND
# COMING

## A SECOND LOOK

## EVANGELIST
## DAVID W. LANKFORD

ISBN 978-0-9896525-3-7

If you are unable to obtain a copy of
*The Second Coming: A Second Look* from your
local bookstore or library, please write or call:

Evangelist David Lankford
The Voice of Evangelism
PO Box 502
Casar, NC 28020
Phone: 704-538-8060

Printed in the United States of America

# DEDICATION

*To my Lord and Saviour,*
*Jesus Christ*
*who has blessed me*
*with revelational knowledge and*
*who has made me what I am*
*and all that I ever hope to be.*
*For I am that I am*
*by the grace of God.*
*To God be the glory.*

.

# CONTENTS

# CHAPTER 1

# A SECOND
# LOOK

K nowing that you are a child of God, you certainly
would want to grow in grace and in knowledge. It is
not my desire to coerce anyone, but to simply share my
experiences, my growth in knowledge in following the
Lord. I am confident the Lord has given me this assign-
ment and I am willing to be obedient to my Master. There
is a Biblical precedent in Paul's willingness to receive revelation from God.

> *But I certify you, brethren, that the gospel which
> was preached of me is not after man. For I nei-
> ther received it of man, neither was I taught it,
> but by the revelation of Jesus Christ. For ye have
> heard of my conversation in time past in the
> Jews' religion, how that beyond measure I per-
> secuted the church of God, and wasted it. And
> profited in the Jews' religion above many of my*

*equals in mine own nation, being more exceedingly zealous of the traditions of my fathers.*

*But when it pleased God, who separated me from my mother's womb, and called me by His grace, to reveal His Son in me, that I might preach Him among the heathen, immediately I conferred not with flesh and blood; neither went I up to Jerusalem to them which were apostles before me, but I went into Arabia, and returned again unto Damascus. Then after three years I went up to Jerusalem to see Peter, and abode with him fifteen days. But other of the apostles saw I none, save James the Lord's brother. Now the things which I write unto you, behold, before God, I lie not* (Galatians 1:11-20).

Paul's gospel that he preached was not after man. This point is of utmost importance because man is fallible. Paul said the gospel he preached, he neither received of man nor was he taught it. It was given by revelation. The Greek word for *taught* means *learn.* It is important to experience things from God and not so much as to be taught it of man.

*But the anointing which ye have received of Him abideth in you, and ye need not that any man teach you; but as the same anointing teacheth you of all things, and is truth, and is no lie, and even as it hath taught you, ye shall abide in Him* (I John 2:27).

Paul received this by absolute revelation of Jesus Christ. When God is ready, He will reveal certain things to us, especially when we are in His place and presence.

In Galatians 1:14, Paul made a profound profession.

He said, *"I am more exceedingly zealous of the traditions of my fathers."* God help us to forsake traditions that are not profitable. *"Beware lest any man spoil you through philosophy and vain deceit, after the tradition of men, after the rudiments of the world, and not after Christ"* (Colossians 2:8). *"This people draweth nigh unto Me with their mouth, and honoureth Me with their lips; but their heart is far from Me. But in vain they do worship Me, teaching for doctrines the commandments of men"* (Matthew 15:8, 9).

In Galatians 1:15–16, Paul spoke of how and when it pleased God to reveal His Son in him. Paul had been born again on the road to Damascus, but there was a need for greater revelation. So, God chose to reveal more to him. God is a God of revelation (I Corinthians 2:9, 10). We may not be willing to admit it, but we are bound and full of traditions that are vain and worthless.

> *Though I might also have confidence in the flesh. If any other man thinketh that he hath whereof he might trust in the flesh, I more: Circumcised the eighth day, of the stock of Israel, of the tribe of Benjamin, a Hebrew of the Hebrews; as touching the law, a Pharisee; concerning zeal, persecuting the church; touching the righteous which is of the law, blameless.*
>
> *But what things were gain to me, those I counted loss for Christ. Yea doubtless, and I count all things but loss for the excellency of the knowledge of Christ Jesus my Lord: for whom I have suffered the loss of all things, and do count them but dung, that I may win Christ. And be found in Him, not having mine own righteousness, which is by God by faith.*
>
> *That I may know Him, and the power of His resur-*

*rection, and the fellowship of His sufferings, being
made conformable unto His death. Not as though
I had already attained, either were already perfect:
but I follow after, if that I may apprehend that for
which also I am apprehended of Christ Jesus.
Brethren, I count not myself to have apprehended: but this one thing I do, forgetting those things
which are behind, and reaching forth unto those
things which are before, I press toward the mark
for the prize of the high calling of God in Christ
Jesus* (Philippians 3:4-16).

Let us examine a man who had everything, yet he
was willing to lose all but the one thing held most valu-
able— Jesus, his Christ. Paul's superiority in the natural (flesh) would exceed that of anyone. Look closely at
verses 5 and 6. Paul met every requirement of Judaism,
being of pure stock and having zeal—he had no superior.

Every advantage Paul had was fleshly (3:7-8). He
had the greatest respect and honor which could be held
among the Jews. But, he counted it ALL loss for the excellent knowledge of Christ. He suffered the loss of all
things, meaning family, associates, brethren, Jewish
tradition, his identity and things already learned and
taught. Without the intention to show disrespect to his
heritage, he counted it all rubbish. Why? To win Christ.
The term *win* (Strong's: Greek #2771) means to *gain
more*. We need to gain more of His excellent knowledge.

Referencing Philippians 3:9, let us all shun our own
righteousness, for it is as filthy rags. God's true righteousness only comes through faith in Jesus. I don't believe the
Church knows Him as we should (3:10). In Verse 12, Paul

said, *"Not as though I have already attained"* (Strong's: Greek # 2658—arrived). To paraphrase, "I haven't arrived myself, neither am I perfect" (Strong's: Greek #5048) or *complete* or *finished*. But, Paul said, I *pursue* (Strong's: Greek #1377), which means *to follow after* Christ, His excellent knowledge, His suffering and His resurrection power. Paul said he did so, *"... that I may apprehend"* (Strong's: Greek # 2638), *to come upon, to seize* the things of God. Paul, no doubt, had not yet seized in experience the fullness of what he was in Christ, yet he was still trying to seize this excellent knowledge which he conceded in Ephesians 3:8 was *unsearchable*. According to Paul, he had a glimpse of glory. In II Corinthians 12·:1-6, he came to visions (Strong's: Greek # 3701), rendered *manifestations* and *revelations* (Strong's: Greek # 602), or *disclosures yet to be revealed* of the things of the Lord. Notice, some things were unlawful for him to utter. [I will speak later about the glory of God that I believe is to yet be revealed or made manifest in the church, His body.]

In Philippians 3:13-14, Paul once again used the term *apprehended* (Strong's: Greek #2638), which meant *to seize or come upon*. Simply put, Paul was saying, *"I have not learned everything or seized everything."* But what was necessary was to forget the past, who he was, what people thought or his future in Judaism. *"I'm reaching forth to the high calling from where Christ is calling me, which is before me."* Let me say, my heart's desire is the same, and I trust the same is true for you as well. And, as He said in I Corinthians 2:9, *"But as it is written, 'Eye hath not seen, nor ear heard, neither have entered into the heart of man, the things which God hath prepared for them that love Him.'"*

In Philippians 3:15-16, Paul said as many be *perfect* (Strong's: Greek #5046), meaning *to be of full age and mature* in Christ. We are to be thus minded with all of the above in mind, and if anyone is otherwise minded, God shall *reveal* (Strong's: Greek #601) this to you, meaning *to take off the cover.*

I have learned through prayer, meditation, consecration and His word, combined with fasting, God will reveal things to us. Paul said in I Corinthians 2:10, that *"the Spirit searcheth all things, yea the deep things of God."* The greatest problem in the Church is spiritual apathy at every level. I am afraid we are just sitting on the sidelines, looking for Jesus to come back. Of course, we are to be looking for His return. But, in so doing, we have stopped growing in grace and knowledge. There is more to God than being saved, sanctified, Holy Ghost baptized and operating in the gifts of the Spirit. There is still more, much more! How do we know? Step out by faith! Trust God; He will prove himself (Deuteronomy 4:29).

> The greatest problem in the Church is spiritual apathy at every level.

Let me say, if you will not give up everything: religion, brethren, and tradition, to suffer the loss of all things willingly, you will not grasp the rest of what I am about to say—and I say this with humility. I understand it is sometimes hard for us to rethink or be retaught some things because we assume we are already correct. With this in mind, allow me to share with you a beautiful story.

One day in the life of Jesus, the people pressed Him to hear His word and Jesus saw two ships standing by the lake. The fishermen had left the ships and were washing their nets. Jesus entered into one of the ships, the one that belonged to Simon Peter, and He requested that Peter thrust out a little from the shore so He could teach the people His word. When He finished His sermon, He said to Peter, *"Launch out,"* (Strong's: Greek #1877) which could be translated *return,* in reference to the *"deep"* (Strong's: Greek #899). Jesus was, I believe, calling Peter, and us, to return to the deep things of God, the *profundities* (Strong's: Greek #899) or *the mysterious things* of God.

At this point, you must remember Jesus was a carpenter, not a fisherman. What could He know? He knew about wood, nails and finishing work—but fishing? He had to be wrong. And like Peter, we often think we already know everything there is to know about a subject. Yet He said, *"Let down* (Strong's: Greek #5465) *your nets* (Strong's: Greek #1350) for a *draught* (Strong's: Greek #61). Jesus was saying, *"Lower your nets into a void or vacancy"* (Strong's: Greek #5465) *"and you will bring in a haul,"* (Strong's: Greek #61).

Often times, when the Spirit of God begins to deal with us and reveal new things to us, we are afraid. Mainly, we are fearful for two reasons: (1) we have never done it that way before and; (2) we are afraid of what will happen to me, myself and I (pride of failure). God help me to be like Peter! *"Master, we have toiled all night and have taken nothing, nevertheless, at Thy word I will let down the net."* How many ministers and ministries feel like they have failed, seen their best days and there is nothing left but to wait on the Lord's return. Essentially, Peter said, Yes, I am a failure. I have devoted a full night's work and have returned empty handed. Still, he obeyed the Master when He gave His word.

The messages and the mysteries of God are still in His Word. When Peter and the others listened and acted on His Word, they *enclosed* (Strong's: Greek #4788) or *embraced* a great multitude of fish. What God reveals and calls us to do will surely be profitable. Peter beckoned unto his *partners* (Strong's: Greek #3353), which could also be rendered *participants or one who shares.* This was a reference to those who were in another boat, that they should come and help. They did come, and both ships were filled so full that both began to sink.

As I read this passage, and I began to understand what God was showing me, I was never more humbled. In Luke 5:8, *"When Simon Peter saw it, he fell down at Jesus' knees, saying, 'Depart from me; for I am a sinful man, O Lord.'"* With this miracle of so many fish, Peter gave vent to his emotion, realizing he had been and was presently wrong about what he thought and about toiling all night. When God shows you something, if you are seeking truth, you are quickly humbled when it is uncovered and you find it.

I understand my unworthiness, for as Paul said, *"I am less than the least of all saints."* Peter and those around him were astonished and amazed at all the fish they had taken in. I believe if we obey His Word, the things God is going to do will astonish everyone.

There are 1,522 *"if's"* in the Bible. All of God's blessings are contingent upon our obedience (John 15:5). Notice what Christ says to Peter, *"Fear not ..."* That is,

*"Don't be afraid to obey My word or believe My words. Trust Me and believe Me and thus you shall catch men."*

God called you to reach people. Yet, you cannot until you launch back out into the deep things of God. And, as in Peter's case, this may even mean doing the same thing you have been doing, yet this time under obedience to God's instruction. When God takes you out into the deep, into the profound mysteries of God, by all means—GO! Go, launch out, and know Him and nothing else, and when you come back to the land, forsake all, follow Him, and win souls for the kingdom of God!

Paul admonished Timothy,

> *And without controversy great is the mystery of godliness. God was manifest in the flesh, justified in the Spirit, seen of angels, preached unto the Gentiles, believed on in the world, received up into glory* (I Timothy 3:16).

And without *controversy* (Strong's: Greek #3672), *great* (Strong's: Greek #373) is the *mystery* (Strong's: Greek #3466) of *godliness* (Strong's: Greek #2150). In the Greek, this passage would read like this: *"Confessedly, without controversy, mighty, strong, exceedingly is the secret of the gospel scheme."* How more powerful a statement could Paul have made? I say, glory to God! Praise the Lord for His unsearchable riches!

I have very prayerfully considered what I am saying and why I have come to a new understanding of the Word of God. Too often, men are afraid to step out in faith. We are comfortable; thus there is no need for a deeper expression of God's presence within our lives. I did not choose this position in life. I was chosen by the King of Glory—I have no choice. God will not repent of His election of me and His call upon my life. Who am I? I am a nobody; a poor earthen vessel who was separated from my mother's womb to carry the greatest possession of all time, The Gospel of Jesus Christ.

# CHAPTER 2

# A NEW
# BEGINNING

After years of what many would call successful ministry, I found myself miserable, frustrated, discontent-
ed, and to be honest, unhappy. Something was missing.
One Sunday morning, after my message to our congregation, out of pure frustration, I made a startling statement, "I will not eat a bite of food until God moves in this
church like I think He should." Dear friend, I never knew
the magnitude of that bold profundity. On the twenty-
first day of my fast, God spoke to me and said that on the
thirty-fifth day, He was going to move in my life and in
our church like I had never before seen.

Although very weak, with great joy, I went to the calendar to mark the day. To my surprise that day fell on a Sunday. Needless to say, I could hardly wait two weeks for the day to arrive. When that blessed Sunday came, the morning service was good, but I did not see that morning what God had promised. Coming home, I told my wife, "I don't understand anything, anymore. I know I heard from God. He promised me He was going to move on the thirty-fifth day." Tired, wounded, wasted and exhausted, I just could not understand.

Then my wife replied, "We still have tonight." She was right. I had already limited God. I returned to church with no sermon, no idea to share, nothing. That night, everything in the service progressed as it had previous Sunday evenings: a couple of songs, the offering, two special musicals, and then it was time for me to enter the pulpit. I still had not thought about a sermon and I did not have an idea or a message prepared. I walked to the pulpit. There I stood, too weak to speak, much less stand and deliver an exhortation. I started to address the congregation. The piano, organ and vocalists were lightly playing and singing beneath the sound of my voice. I said, "I just want to worship the Lord. Would everyone please lift your hands and worship God." After a minute or so, I asked the singers to stop singing, even though they were barely making a sound. Another few moments passed and I looked at the pianist and motioned for the musicians to stop playing.

A holy hush fell all over the building. In the silence, I looked across the room. Suddenly, I noticed a haze. A whitish blue cloud began to fill the sanctuary. Some say they saw fire. Others saw what I did. Then the power of God smote me almost violently. I felt as though I was going to explode. I felt as though, if God did not release me, turn me loose, I was going to physically die. I honestly remember hurting physically, for God's power was more than I could bear. My eyes were opened. I saw the tabernacle and I got a quick glimpse of the Holy of Holies. I saw "the glory" or at least a measure of God's glory. I know it was but for a moment, yet I immediately knew I had been brought to a dimension, a level, to which I had never been in my life.

I believe God showed me why there are cherubim on the Ark of the Covenant. They go before Him and make a path of holiness whereby He may walk down with absolutely no distractions; for He is the King of Glory. No one and nothing will distract His coming and when His presence comes in this measure, it is nothing less than pure glory. That night was a night unparalleled in my life. I knew I would never be the same.

I completed the remainder of the forty-day fast, not knowing that only a short time afterward I would attend our denominational state camp meeting at which Doug Small would be teaching on the Tabernacle. I was helped tremendously by his message, for I admit that I really knew very little on the subject prior to his teaching. I obtained his materials and began to study and pray—not knowing what God was preparing to do to me.

During my fast, God told me to quit counting our people. At that time, I could not understand. He gave me I Chronicles 21:1 as a scripture of reference. After reading it and taking its message to heart, I quit counting. Before I could fully accept what God had told me, a slow and gradual mass exodus began in our church. No church disagreements; no problems at all. People just quit coming, moved and changed churches. There were no apparent reasons for their departure—the people and the numbers were just gone.

My frustrations mounted. I had just had a glimpse of the glory of God, and the next thing He tells me is, stop counting, and then our church starts disappearing. Everything should have been getting better, yet they were worse than before God started moving in my life. I got so angry with my situation I started to go on another forty day fast. Yet, after praying one evening, I got up from my knees and the Holy Ghost said to me, "Don't fast, just pray." I became a praying man.

I went six months, never missing a day in prayer. Sometimes I even prayed two or three times a day. I began to beg God for some kind of deliverance from this discouraging situation in our church. One night in prayer at the church, I begged God for at least a word from the scripture. I asked, "God, when I open the Bible, wherever it falls open, please give me a word." I knew what happened had to be of God for there before my eyes was Jeremiah 18:6, *"Behold, as the clay is in the potter's hand, so are ye in mine hand."*

I was happy and relieved to hear from God, yet I felt He was almost being cruel to me. Still, I knew He loved me. It often hurts to be in God's hands. About two months passed. Then one day while at home, the Holy Ghost said, "Go to I Peter and start reading." In the first twelve verses, I had most of my answers about what God was trying to teach me. It had to do with the last days before Christ's return, and about the glory of God. From that moment, my mind was cleansed, my joy was restored, and my frustration immediately ceased. I was at a place where God could now reveal to me what He wanted me to understand.

Let me say, I have been tried by His fire and holiness. All of this has brought me to the place I presently hold in His Spirit. There are two other points I should make before we move on. First, I had asked some questions of myself prior to all of this: "Had I seen my best days? Were my greatest days in the ministry behind me?" I concluded I did not know, but I would be faithful, no matter what.

The second point involves a dear sister in the Lord. On Sunday, October 1, 1995, a lady in our church gave me a word, saying, "Your best days are yet ahead of you." She continued to relate to me God was preparing me for a work in the End Times and my ministry had not even begun its climb. Many works lay before me and doors and spiritual levels were yet to be experienced. Without question, the word she related was a great encouragement.

The next day, I went to Asheville North Carolina, to visit with my dad. I had with me another pastor who wanted to stop and visit a friend whom I also knew. When we got to this friend's home, I began to share with him some of my new revelation knowledge. Immediately, he stopped me and said, "I have a word for you. The Spirit began to say, 'For some time I have been stripping you of things, close friends, and others around you, for I have been positioning you for quite some time to do a work in your life.'" There was no way this person could have known my ups and downs. No way could he have known about the loss of close and intimate friendships within our church—and for absolutely no reason. It was as though my life became shrouded with absolute mystery, yet the Holy Ghost was enacting a work in my life like I had never known.

It is very hard to share with you my feelings at that time, for they were frustrated and totally unbearable. I could hardly stand anything, anymore. Still, when a man knows he is called of God, what else can he do but submit to the work of God in his life? We often plead with God to move and work in our lives. Yet, when He tries, we resist because, in the realm of ordinary thinking, it appears to be obscured. A Spirit-filled man with a pure heart will not be deceived and fall into heresy because the great Holy Ghost will not allow that to happen.

Six days later, on October 8, while I was driving to church, the Holy Ghost spoke a word to my heart. "I have yet many things to say to you. But, you are not able to bear them." These words kept repeating in my mind. As soon as I got to church, I went to my *Strong's Concordance* to find this verse and there it was. John 16:12, 13 says,

> *I have yet many things to say to you, but ye cannot bear them now. Howbeit, when He, the Spirit of Truth, is come, He will guide you into all truth; for He shall not speak of Himself, but whatsoever He shall hear that shall He speak; and He shall show you things to come.*

Finnis J. Dake says that the term *bear* in verse 12 means to *carry* or *bear what is burdened.* In other words, in this context, it means to not be able to understand a matter or receive it calmly. Needless to say, it has been hard to bear and receive these things calmly. It will do you good to remember these verses as you read and consider the

ideas in the following pages. Remember the promise, "...
*and He shall show you things to come.*"

# CHAPTER 3

# THE GLORY
# OF GOD

In my spirit, I know, if you will be honest, many of you are miserable—as miserable in your pursuit of truth as I was. Sometimes you are so irritable that you don't know what to do or how to handle situations that arise. I'll tell you the reason you are so miserable: Something is missing. That's right! Something is missing. You say, "I'm saved, sanctified, Holy Ghost baptized, and even operating in the gifts." Yet, there is more, much more. It's the Glory of God.

If we examine ourselves, are we in the condition that Ephesians 5:27 says of the Church, the people of God, who He will present to Himself? Where is the Glory? Where is the glorious power with which the Church should be operating? I will discuss the Glory of the Church later.

Let us talk briefly about the Tabernacle. There is the Outer Court, the Holy Place, and the Most Holy Place. I believe the church, the denomination in which I grew up, and so many others, perhaps most, are operating in either the Holy Place or the Outer Court. We are wandering like the nation of Israel in Acts 7:38, where Stephen speaks of *"the church that was in the wilderness."* I am convinced our frustrations are so paramount because we have lived in the Holy Place or Outer Court for over 100 years and it is time to move into the Most Holy Place. We are being prepared to move into the place where there is no light (Menorah) or shew bread. Yet, in this Most Holy Place, there is light (John 8:12) and there is bread (John 6:35). There is everything, for therein lies the Glory of God.

There is no need for any natural substance; for the Glory of God is there to sustain us. Moses neither ate nor drank for 80 days (Deut. 9:9-21). He lived off the presence of God. I believe God wants to move the Church into this Most Holy Place to receive more abundantly from Him. And then, He will come back.

We must remember, when God wants to do a new work, it will create division with many. In the late 1800's, many knew there was more of God to be known and a deeper walk with God, which was the experience in the Holy Ghost. Yet, the new work of the Holy Ghost divided homes, families, churches and denominations. I'm willing to suffer in order that the Spirit and power and the Glory of God may rest upon me. Just like Paul, if I must needs glory, I will glory in the things which concern my infirmities (II Corinthians 11:30). When a man walks in the Spirit, what shall he fear? For, He hath said, *"I will never leave nor forsake thee."* So we may boldly say that the Lord is my helper and I will not fear what man shall do unto me (Hebrews 13:5, 6).

The Lord Jesus Christ will come again, yet the Church has one more spiritual step to take before He does. I trust from this moment on, you will have an open heart and mind to the things which the Spirit may be saying to you. I would even encourage you to take a moment for sincere prayer, asking that He, the Christ of God, would speak to your heart. He is no respecter of persons. I believe there are scores of others who will relate and understand my words, for they will bear witness. Remember I John 4:1, *"Beloved, believe not every spirit, but try the spirits whether they are of God."*

Too long we foolishly have thought we have God and His Word entirely figured out. I am here to tell you, WE DON'T! We present Christ to a dying world through a tenet, a manifesto, a dogma, when His riches are unsearchable. And when the Church becomes filled with tepidity, we lose the greatness and the glory of God's expression in our lives. God bless you as you read on. I haven't figured it all out. I, too, am still seeking. I am, however, prepared to flow in His direction and move according to His leadership.

For nearly 60 years, we have been at a virtual stand still, wandering around in the wilderness and going nowhere. I believe the last real move of God involved the Faith Healing Movement that came to prominence in the middle of the twentieth century, epitomized by men like Oral Roberts, who God used to reach far beyond the classical Pentecostal movement. During that time, there were great tent meetings with hundreds being healed. It was a marvelous time. Yet, what have we seen since?

Yes, I am well aware of the Charismatic movement. I was even a part of it throughout the 1980's. I remember being in New York and having prayer lines with hundreds of gatherers falling all over the place. There were times God used me to minister in the Holy Ghost's slaying of the

> Tribulation, coupled with persecution, brings about the Glory of God.

people. But, there were also times when people fell at my hand and I knew it was not real—the Holy Ghost did not slay them. When you are a man of God, you know when it's real and when it's not.

Yes, I have witnessed all of the great things in the Charismatic movement. Yet, one must agree there has not been a perpetual move of the Holy Ghost in over 60 years. Holiness is a prerequisite of the divine move of the power of God (See Joshua 3:5). We are truly on the verge of something beyond our comprehension. It will not be for everyone, only those who press into His holy presence (Psalm 91:1) will experience it. This that I speak of will be the element which God uses to bring forth the Church through all that it must face.

Tribulation, coupled with persecution, brings about the Glory of God. The Church must be made glorious for the divine presentation at His coming. As we presently know, the Church you will soon see a definite divine move of God Almighty. Get prepared for the Holy

THE GLORY OF GOD

Remnant—simply put, for the saints of God who are about to enter the Holy of Holies. Once the Church enters into the Holy of Holies, we need not fear any detriment or loss, for God's glory will sustain the Church during the forthcoming days. Hold on to Christ and live in His divine presence. For only by His power, might and glory shall we overcome. John 17:22 says, *"And the Glory which Thou gavest Me I have given them."*

I can personally say I am living more, day by day, in the Holy of Holies. So, I have no fear or insecurities about what lies before me. If you are really living a holy and dedicated life you will soon begin to experience the New Testament Glory of God. I can promise you that.

# CHAPTER 4

# THE
# RAPTURE

Before I began to write on this topic, I attempted a historical background check of the denominational minutes of the church where I grew up, a classical Pentecostal denomination. After conferring with Pentecostal historian, Dr. Charles Conn, I continued to pursue the matter. In 1910, a study of the Rapture was made by our early Pentecostal forefathers. However, records were not kept. Nor were there any absolutes determined or committed to writing at that time.

Then in 1948, a statement regarding eschatology became a part of the Declaration of Faith that was adopted and placed in the General Assembly Minutes (Church of God). The statement said we believe, "In the premillennial second coming of Jesus. First, to resurrect the righteous dead and to catch away the living saints to Him in the air. Second, to reign on the earth a thousand years." The position is not definitively that of a pre-tribulation rapture, but of Classical Pre-millennialism. And that position has a number of variations with respect to "the rapture"—pre-tribulation, mid-tribulation, pre-wrath, post-tribulation. However, these early Pentecostals chose not to rigidly define their eschatology.

I personally believe that if our church forefathers had been adamant about the sequence: a "rapture first" followed by a "seven-year tribulation," and a later Second Advent, they would have defined their eschatology to reflect that belief. However, they never used the term *rapture*. Instead, they used the phrase *premillennial second coming*. They, in fact, left an open door for more widely held eschatological views within the premillennialist perspective. That convinces me of their wisdom. They were both prudent and spiritual leaders.

General Assemblies of most denominations were created for the express purpose of discussing the scriptures. Yet, few do much of this anymore. This lack of analysis of and focus on the scriptures is most likely a contributing factor in our wandering around in the wilderness for the last fifty years. We are so concerned with programs, policies and procedures that we miss what God is saying and what the Holy Ghost is trying to accomplish. The Holy Spirit prompted me to quit relying on commentaries and to strictly interpret the Scriptures by the Scriptures because the Word of God is *God-breathed, God-inspired* and infallible.

**If we cannot concur on this, stop reading now—
for all I will share from this point forward is Bible—
the Word of God as interpreted by the Word of God.**

So, does the Bible clearly point out a rapture and then
seven years later a Second Advent? Well, let us first look
at I Thessalonians 4:13-18. Closely examine the words of
Paul without prior assumptions, and don't take away anything from the text.

> *But, I would not have you be ignorant, brethren,
> concerning them which are asleep, that ye sorrow
> not, even as others which have no hope. For if we
> believe that Jesus died and rose again, even so them
> also which sleep in Jesus will God bring with Him.
> For this we say unto you by the word of the Lord,
> that we which are alive and remain unto the com-
> ing of the Lord shall not prevent them which are
> asleep. For the Lord Himself shall descend from
> heaven with a shout, with the voice of the arch-
> angel, and with the trump God: and the dead in
> Christ shall rise first: Then we which are alive and
> remain shall be caught up together with them in
> the clouds, to meet the Lord in the air: and so shall
> we ever be with the Lord. Wherefore comfort one
> another with these words.* (I Thessalonians 4:13-
> 18).

Notice Paul's concern, *"I would not have you be
ignorant."* I want you to understand the things concerning them which are asleep. He also said we are not to be
grieved, as other people who have no *hope* or *confidence*
(Strong's: Greek #1680) in life beyond this life. Notice
verse 14: *"For if we believe that Jesus died and rose again*

*even so them also which sleep in Jesus will God bring with Him."* We believe that the dead in Christ are already in heaven, awaiting the resurrection day when they will receive that glorified body.

> *Therefore we are always confident, knowing that, whilst we are at home in the body, we are absent from the Lord. For we walk by faith, not by sight. We are confident, I say, and willing to be absent from the body, and to be present with the Lord* (II Corinthians 5:6-8).

I believe I Thessalonians 4:14 is a partial fulfillment of Revelation 19:14; namely, that God will bring with Him the saints already in heaven— *"This we say unto you by the Word of the Lord that we which are alive and remain unto the "coming" of the Lord shall not prevent them which are asleep."* Notice the word *coming* (Strong's: Greek #3952). Strong says, it is *"the advent of Christ;"* specifically to punish Jerusalem and finally the wicked. In this case, Paul is not speaking of a rapture, but specifically of the Second Advent of Christ to punish and destroy the wicked. Note verse 16: *"For the Lord Himself,"* not another, but *the Lord Himself, "shall descend* (Strong's: Greek #2597). It means *to crack open or cause to burst asunder–* and, of course, it is the heavens. This descent from Heaven is with a *shout* (Strong's: Greek #2752). That is also used of *a cry of excitement* or even *a military command.* And it is with the voice of the *Archangel* (Strong's: Greek #743), *the chief angel* and with the trump of God. The result is that the dead (Strong's: Greek #3498), the *corpse of the deceased* believers in Christ shall rise first. Do we see a descent, followed by an ascension (the rapture), followed by yet another descent (the second coming)? No, we do not. Yet, those who hold to a pre-tribulation rapture separate the second coming into these two stages. Nowhere is this taught in the scriptures. His first coming was in one stage (the incarnation), and so will be His second coming.

Notice verse 17: *"Then we which are alive and remain shall be caught up* (Strong's: Greek #1726), the term means *to seize or to catch away by force.* We will be caught up together in the clouds, *"to meet the Lord in the air and so shall we ever be with the Lord."* Now, the passage does not say anything about us going to heaven. It only says we are caught up to meet the Lord in the *air* (Strong's: Greek #109), which is naturally *circumambient.* This term *air* is precisely the same word Paul used in I Corinthians 9:26, *"I therefore, so run not as uncertainly; so fight I, not as one that beateth the air,"* literally, the air that surrounds us. Nowhere does the passage speak of us going to heaven. Rather, it says we will have an encounter with the Lord in the air.

Let's go systematically through I Thessalonians 5.

- Verse 1: *"But of the 'times'"* (Strong's: Greek #5550). This refers to 'a space of time that is distinguished, which designates a fixed or special occasion'; and seasons (Strong's: Greek #2540), which is an occasion set or a proper time. You have no need that I write (Strong's: Greek #1125) or that I describe this unto you.

- Verse 2: *"For you yourselves know"* (Strong's: Greek #1492), that is, you perceive or understand

and do so perfectly (Strong's: Greek #199) or 'exactly', *"that the day of the Lord"'* (Strong's: Greek #2962), the one who is supreme in authority, the controller *"so cometh as a thief in the night."*

- Verse 3: *"For when they shall say peace and safety,"*—notice closely that Paul declares the destruction to be at them, to affect specifically those who say *"peace and safety,"* not God's people. And then—*"sudden destruction"* (Strong's: Greek #3639) comes, meaning ruin, to be destroyed, punishment, even death. And it *"cometh upon them as travail"* (Strong's: Greek #5608), which means *to experience the pains of parturition,* of child birth upon a woman, and the Scripture declares, *"and they shall not escape."*

  Notice all destruction and travail are directed at they and them, meaning *"those who say peace and safety"* and not the discerning church.

- Verse 4: *"But ye, brethren, are not in darkness"* (Strong's: Greek #4655); or you are not in obscurity. *"That day"* will not *overtake you* (Strong's: Greek #2698), which means to *seize or catch you* *"as a thief"* would, by surprise.

  *"That day"* is the coming of the Lord and Paul does not distinguish between a rapture and a subsequent Second Advent. If the church is raptured out of the earth, and we are not here, why does Paul say, *"That day of destruction should not overtake us as a thief?"* It is because we will still be

here on the earth. We are warned not to allow the day of destruction to come upon us as it would a thief. For when they, the men of the world, those around us, cry peace and safety, that is a sign to us that destruction is near.

- Verse 5: *"Ye are all the "children"* (Greek 5207), *that is, 'sons' ... "of light and the children of day."* We are not of the night or of darkness. We read in I John 3:1, *"What manner of love the Father hath bestowed upon us that we should be called the sons of God."* In Roman 8:14, Paul said, *"For as many as are led by the spirit of God, they are the sons of God."*

- Verse 9: *"For God hath not appointed us to wrath"* (Strong's: Greek #3709), that is to *punishment* or an experience of *indignation* but to *obtain* (Strong's: Greek #4047), which means *to become the purchased possession* in this case, of the Lord, to *"obtain salvation by our Lord Jesus Christ."*

God will preserve His Church, His purchased possession for which He died. Look at Paul's comments in Ephesians 1:13, 14:

> *In whom ye also trusted, after that ye heard the word of truth, the gospel of your salvation: in whom, also after that ye believed, ye were sealed with that Holy Spirit of promise, which is the earnest of our inheritance until the redemption of the purchased possession, unto the praise of his glory.*

The word *sealed* (Strong's: Greek #4972) indicates

a *stamp for security*—a sealing *"with that Holy Spirit"* Himself, a sealing that which contains a promise. This is the *earnest* (Strong's: Greek #728), *the pledge or down payment,* the assuring of our *inheritance* (Strong's: Greek #2817), of our *possession.*

I know this may be difficult for you to grasp, but please listen to what Paul is saying. The Day of Destruction is not to take us unaware. In Luke 21:34, we read, *"And take heed to yourselves, lest at any time, your hearts be overcharged with surfeiting, and drunkenness, and cares of this life, and so that day come upon you unawares."*

Let us now go to II Thessalonians 1:4, *"So that we ourselves glory in you, in the churches of God, for your patience and faith in all you persecutions and tribulations that ye endure"* (Strong's: Greek #430), that you put up with persecutions and tribulations.

Notice verse 5: *"Which is a manifest token of the righteous judgment of God."* Notice three terms: token, the righteous, and judgment. The word *token* (Strong's: Greek #1780-1922) means that which is *instrumentally, constructive* of the *righteous* (Strong's: Greek #1342). Here it is a reference to God's action, which is the *right* or *upright* thing to do, the righteous *judgment* (Strong's: Greek #2920), an expression of the *justice,* the righteous act of God. That ye may be counted worthy of the kingdom of God, for which ye also *suffer* (Strong's: Greek #3958), a reference to *life experiences.* Remember the words of our Lord, *"Watch ye therefore, and pray always, that ye may be accounted worthy to escape all these things that shall come to pass, and to stand before the Son of Man"* (Luke 21:36).

What we are going through, as well as what we are about

to go through, will be allowed by God. God is judging the Church this very moment in preparation for His final judgment at His appearing. II Timothy 4:1 declares, *"I charge thee therefore before God and the Lord Jesus Christ, who shall judge the quick and the dead at his appearing."* The term *judge* (Strong's: Greek #2929) is to *determine* or *decide*; in this case, regarding the quick and *dead* (Strong's: Greek #2198), which can be translated *corpse* at His *appearing* (Strong's: Greek #2015), specifically, the *advent of Christ* and His kingdom.

> When He comes again it will be to resurrect the dead in Christ, catch away the living to meet the Lord in the air, and then establish an earthly kingdom.

Yes, you read that right. God will pass final judgment on the Church, the dead and living, at His appearing and kingdom. So, we are to preach the Word. Christ will not tolerate compromise. Here again, Paul does not differentiate between a rapture and a Second Advent. It simply reads *"at His appearing and kingdom."* When He comes again, it will be to resurrect the dead in Christ, catch away the living to meet the Lord Himself in the air, and then establish an earthly kingdom.

Many ministers and Christians today are frustrated by their many trials, tribulation and persecutions. The reason for these hardships is because we are being judged now for final judgment which will be determined at His coming. Remember the words of our Lord in Revelation 22: 12, *"And behold, I come quickly and My reward is with Me to give every man according as his work shall be."* At His coming, we will judged and rewarded. We are in an earthly trial here on the earth like that of the Thessalonians who were suffering great tribulation and persecution.

Why? So we may be accounted worthy of the kingdom of God, *"for which ye also suffer."* Do not be discouraged. You are about to inherit the kingdom of God at His appearing and kingdom. Trials and persecutions must happen so He can present to Himself a glorious Church. One day soon, it will be worth it all. Paul said in II Timothy 2:12, *"If we suffer, we shall also reign with Him."* Romans 8:18, *"For I reckon that the sufferings of the present time are not worthy to be compared with the Glory which shall be revealed in us"* (future tense). Praise God! I am counted worthy to suffer shame for His name; for He has promised to be with us until the end and the end is very near. We have to be tried so as to be made pure.

Daniel 12:9, 10 reads,

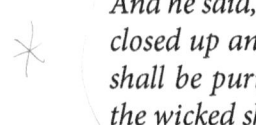

> *And he said, 'Go thy way, Daniel: for the words are closed up and sealed to the time of the end. Many shall be purified, and made white, and tried, but the wicked shall do wickedly and none of the wicked shall understand· but the wise shall understand.*

Daniel was told to seal up the words until the time of the end, which is now.

We are those living at the end and must be tried to be made pure and white. Daniel said the wicked shall not understand, but the wise shall understand. Remember, the words of Peter in I Peter 4:17, *"For the time is come that judgment must begin at the house of God: and if it first begin at us, what shall the end be of them that obey not the gospel of God?"* This again proves we, the Church, are having to be judged first in order that final judgment may be passed at His appearing. Peter said, *"What shall be the end to them who obey not the gospel of God."* Paul again answers that in II Thessalonians 1:8, *"... in flaming fire, taking vengeance on them that know not God and that obey not the gospel of our Lord Jesus Christ."* We need not fear being tried. It will complete or perfect us, and make us what we should be for Christ.

I will get back to our discussion of the rapture shortly, but it is necessary to understand why we are presently being tried. In I Peter 4:12 13, Peter said, *"Beloved, think it not strange"* (Strong's: Greek #3579), something foreign *"concerning the fiery trial"* (Strong's: Greek #1383), the testing *"which is to try you"* (Strong's: Greek #3986) to *scrutinize* or *examine* you. It is not, Peter suggests, *"As though some unexpected strange* (Strong's: Greek #3579) *or foreign and unusual thing had happened to you—it is expected. So rejoice, inasmuch as ye are partakers"* (Strong's: Greek #2841) *"among those who share Christ's sufferings, that when His glory shall be revealed"* (Strong's: Greek #602), *"that is, at His appearing or coming ye may be glad also with exceeding joy."*

Here again, Peter does not differentiate between a rapture and a Second Advent. What he does say is that we must be tried as though with fire, to be found worthy at His appearing. Paul said in I Corinthians. 3:13, *"Every man's work"* (Strong's: Greek #201) his deeds or acts shall be manifest, for the day—the day of the Lord—shall declare it, because it shall be *revealed* (Strong's: Greek #601), *disclosed* or *uncovered by fire.* And the fire shall try every man's work of what sort it is. Remember, he comes in flaming fire.

Paul, in I Corinthians 3:14, says *"If anyone's work which he has built on it endures, he will receive a reward."* A man's work or deeds abide if he has built upon the foundation of Jesus Christ. That man shall receive a reward. Revelation 22:12 says, *"And, behold: I come quickly; and My reward is with Me, to give every man according as his work shall be."* You see, our crown is being laid up for us right now as we endure and suffer.

> *"For I am now ready to be offered, and the time of my departure is at hand. I have fought a good fight, I have finished my course, I have kept the faith: Henceforth, there is laid up for me a crown of righteousness, which the Lord, the righteous judge, shall give me at that day: and not to me only, but unto all them also that love his appearing (II Timothy 4:6-8).*

Read verse 8 closely, *"Henceforth, there is laid up for me a crown of righteousness which the Lord the righteous judge shall give me at that day."* What day? The day when He judges the quick and dead at His appearing and kingdom (II Timothy 4:1). Yet he said, *"... not to me only, but unto all them that love His appearing'* (Strong's: Greek #2015), the Second Advent of Christ. Again, there is no differentiation between a rapture and Second Advent.

I believe God is about to allow great trouble to come upon the world and the church, like we have never seen before.

Now, let's go back to II Thessalonians 1:6 and look more closely at what Paul had to say about the Thessalonians who were suffering and looking for the return of Christ. We are all aware Paul's second letter was to help clarify to the Thessalonians the teaching which was circulating in that day, that the resurrection was a fallacy. What we must understand from II Thessalonians 1:5-6 is that God is willfully allowing tribulation to come into the lives of the Thessalonians and so it is in our lives. I believe God is about to allow great trouble to come upon the world and the church, like we have never seen before. Remember, God makes it rain on the just and the unjust (Matthew 5:45). In Revelation 3:10-11 we read,

> *Because that thou hast kept the word of my patience, I also will keep thee from the hour of temptation which shall come upon all the world to try them that dwell upon the earth. Behold, I come quickly, hold that fast that thou hast that no man take thy crown.*

The term *try* (Strong's: Greek #3985) means *to prove*. In this passage, we see all will be tried or tested on the entire planet. But we need not fear, because Revelation 12:11 says that "*... they overcame him by the blood of the Lamb and by the word of their testimony and they loved not their lives unto death.*" So, no matter what we face, we will overcome.

In I John and also in Revelation, the word *overcometh* is used a total of eleven times. I want to be an overcomer. In Revelation 3:11, Jesus urges,

> *Hold fast to your crown,*" and II Timothy 4:8, Paul said, "*There is laid up for me a crown of righteousness, which the Lord, the righteous judge, shall give*

*me at that day: and not to me only, but unto all them also that love His appearing.*

The crown is yours. Just hold fast until He comes for He brings His reward with Him.

Now looking back at II Thessalonians 1:7 we read, *"And you who are troubled, rest with us, when the Lord Jesus shall be revealed from heaven with His mighty angels."* Look closely, His coming is with angels. Angels announced His first coming in Luke 2:10-14 and they will come with Him at His second coming. Read these verses closely. Notice how important it will be for angels to be with Him at His second coming. Here again, there is no differentiation in a rapture or the Second Advent.

> *He answered and said unto them, He that sowed the good seed is the Son of Man; the field is the world, the good seed are the children of the kingdom, but the tares are the children of the wicked one; the enemy that soweth them is the devil, the harvest is the end of the world; and the reapers are the angels. As therefore the tares are gathered and burned in the fire; so shall it be in the end of this world. The Son of Man shall send forth His angels, and they shall gather out of his kingdom all things that offend, and them which do iniquity. And shall cast them in to a furnace of fire: there shall be wailing and gnashing of teeth. Then shall the righteous shine forth as the sun in the kingdom of their Father. Who hath ears to hear, let him hear* (Matthew 13:37-43).

In this passage we see that the good seed are the children of God. The tares are of the wicked one. The reapers are the angels. The angels gather out of His kingdom all that offend and those which do iniquity. Then shall the righteous shine. In Matthew 16:27, the Bible declares, *"For the Son of Man shall come in the glory of His Father with His angels, and then He shall reward every man according to his works."* Revelation 22:12 says, *"And, behold, I come quickly, and My reward is with Me, to give every man according as his work shall be."* The rapture and Second Advent are the same event.

Matthew 24:31 states, *"And He shall send His angels with a great sound of a trumpet, and they shall gather His elect from the four winds, from one end of heaven to the other."* Here in this passage, Matthew speaks of a trumpet, a great sound which will wake the dead in Christ. I Corinthians 15:51–52 declares,

> *Behold, I show you a mystery, we shall not all sleep, but we shall all be changed, in a moment, in the twinkling of an eye, at the last trump; for the trumpet shall sound, and the dead shall be raised incorruptible, and we shall be changed.*

In I Thessalonians. 4:16, Paul declares, *"For the Lord Himself shall descend from heaven with a shout, with the voice of the archangel, and with the trump of God: and the dead in Christ shall rise first."* Hallelujah! The trumpet is sure to sound. I hope you are ready. In Matthew 24:36, notice also that the angels do not know when or what time this will occur.

In Matthew 25:31, we notice how Christ will come in glory, *"When the Son of man shall come in His glory, and all the holy angels with Him, then shall He sit upon the throne of His glory."* I see no secret in His coming. Paul spoke of His glorious appearing in Titus 2:13. And again, in all of these Scriptures there is no differentiation in a rapture and a Second Advent. II Thessalonians 1:8 states, *"In flaming fire taking vengeance on them that know not God, and that obey not the gospel of Lord Jesus Christ."* I think it is important we recognize there is the same and everlasting punishment for both factions: (1) those who know not God and (2) those who obey not the gospel.

One group knows the gospel, yet fails to obey it; while the other group doesn't even know God. Verse 9 says, *"[They] shall be punished with everlasting destruction from the presence of the lord, and from the glory of His power."* They will be punished with everlasting destruction from His presence. How long is everlasting? Well, the punishment will last forever. To continue, verse 10 says, *"When He shall come to be glorified in His saints, and to be admired in all them that believe in that day,"* because, Paul says, our testimony among you was believed in that day. When He comes to be *glorified* (Strong's: Greek #1740) or to be *recognized for all that He is*, it will be among or in His *saints* (Strong's: Greek #40), those *consecrated* to Him—He will be admired in all them that believe. Here again, in this passage, it says nothing about us leaving and going to heaven, but that He will come and be glorified or recognized in His saints who are here on the earth.

Now let us look at II Thessalonians 2:1, *"Now we beseech you, brethren, by the coming of our Lord Jesus Christ, and by our gathering together unto Him."* Paul beseeches or implores the brethren, by the *coming* (Strong's: Greek #3952) as *to a place,* of our Lord Jesus Christ and then, by our *gathering together* (Strong's: Greek #1997), *as-*

*sembling together* at one place unto Him, which is some place in the air, of both the dead and the living, to the meeting that Paul spoke of in I Thessalonians 4:17. Once again, there is no differentiation in a rapture or a Second Advent. In verse 2, *"That ye be not soon shaken in mind, or be troubled, neither by spirit, nor by word, nor by letter as from us, as the day of Christ is at hand."*

We are not to allow anything to trouble us for the day of Christ is *at hand* (Strong's: Greek #1764) which means *to come in an instant*. This reminds me of Peter's words in I Peter 4:7, *"But the end of all things is at hand, be ye therefore sober, and watch unto prayer."* Notice II Thessalonians 2:3, *"Let no man deceive you by any means"* (Strong's: Greek #5158), by any mode or by way of style, *"For that day will not come!"* What day? The day Paul was speaking of in II Thessalonians 2:1, *"the coming of our Lord Jesus Christ, and by our gathering together unto Him."* Notice that once again, there is no differentiation between a rapture and a Second Advent.

Before He comes, there will *come* (Strong's: Greek #2064) *a falling away* first. The term *come* denotes motion from one place to another. In other words, people leaving their spiritual post, departing from the faith. That's why Paul said, *"Let no one deceive you."* That day—the day of His return—will not take place until there is a *falling away* (Strong's: Greek #646). The phrase *falling away* is very much misunderstood. It is the Greek word *apostasia* which means to defect or forsake, literally to depart from the faith.

Some Bible scholars teach that *apostasia*, which means *departure*, but typically only in a secondary sense; the primary meaning is to become an apostate with regard to faith, to depart from a position of belief. However, some interpret this to mean our departure from the earth, and thus the rapture. If that is the case, then let us insert the word *rapture* into this verse. *"Let no man deceive you by any means for the* [rapture] *shall not come except there come a* [rapture] *first; and the man of sin be revealed, the son of perdition."* I don't mean to be funny, but that makes no sense at all. So, the term *apostasia* would have to mean a "departing from the faith." In the Greek, according to *Strong's Exhaustive Concordance*, it carries the concept of separation, synonymous with a *divorcement* (Strong's: Greek #647). We will not be departing, separating or divorcing from Christ, but we will be gathering unto Him.

> During the days of Noah, a total of eleven souls were saved.

In I Timothy 4:1, Paul spoke of Christians departing from the faith. In that passage the phrase "falling away" means those who would reject Christ. Here in America, we see fewer and fewer people come to the saving grace and knowledge of Jesus. There are revivals, and I mean true revival, in particular parts of the world, but not in America. Jesus said, *"As it was in the days of Noah and Lot, so shall it be also in the coming of the Son of Man."* During the days of Noah and Lot, a total of eleven souls were saved. It would have been twelve, but Lot's wife looked back (Genesis 19:26). As we will see, more people will apostatize and reject Christ. Paul said, first there will be a great rejection of Christ and then the man of sin will be *revealed* (Strong's: Greek #602) or *disclosed.* He is the lawless one, the son of perdition (Strong's:

Greek #684), or the one who brings destruction and waste.

II Thessalonians 2:4 speaks about this man of sin, *"[He] who opposeth and exalteth himself above all that is called God, or that is worshiped; so that he as God sitteth in the temple of God, showing himself that he is God."* This verse is very descriptive of the character of the Antichrist. Notice verse 5, *"Remember ye not, that, when I was yet with you, I told these things?"* I want to ask you a question. If we are not to be here, why should we be told in Thessalonians, along with the Thessalonians, for the Word is not only for them, but also for us—to remember these things? Verses 2 and 3 declare,

> *That ye be not soon shaken in mind, or be troubled, neither by spirit, nor by word, nor by letter as from us, as that the day of Christ is at hand. Let no man deceive you by any means: for that day shall not come, except there come a falling away first, and that man of sin be revealed, the son of perdition.*

They were told not to be troubled by spirit, word or letter because Christ's return was still at hand, the resurrection had not passed, as some were reporting. They were also told to remember there would be a falling away in which many would reject Christ, that they should remember when they see this man of sin in the temple, exalting himself, as if he were God. When that occurred, then the coming of Christ was very near.

The term *remember* (Strong's: Greek #3421), means to exercise the memory, to recollect, to rehearse or to be mindful. If the church is not here on the earth when this happens, why write these things to the Church

and then tell them, the Thessalonians, and by exten-
sion us, to exercise our memory when these things
begin to happen. In verse 6 we discover, *"And now ye
know what withholdeth"* (Strong's: Greek #2722) or
restrains that he might be revealed (Strong's: Greek
#602) or disclosed in his time (Strong's: Greek #2540).

The term *time* here means a time which gives one an
opportunity. So he, the man of sin, will have his time
and opportunity, which will be 42 months, to do all of
his blasphemies. Revelation 13:5 reads, *"And there was
given unto him a mouth speaking great things and blasphemies, and power was given unto him to continue forty
and two months."* God will allow time for him; in fact,
the man of sin's time. This time is synonymous with
Luke 22:53 which reads, *"When I was daily with you
in the temple, ye stretched forth no hands against me:
but this is your hour [time], and the power of darkness."*

The time must be given to the Antichrist. Paul told the
Thessalonians, you know what is "withholding." If they
knew, why can't we know? My beloved mentor, Finis J.
Dake, who I respect and esteem highly, asks the same
question. And with humility of mind and heart, I disagree
with his viewpoint (*Dake's Bible*, p. 230, col. 2, 'the hinderer
of lawlessness'). In II Thessalonians 2:7, *"For the mystery
of iniquity doth already work: only he who now letteth will
let, until he be taken out of the way."* Dake says one of three
things will be removed: government, the Church or the
Holy Spirit. My disagreement with Dake's view is that he
says the restraining dynamic is "taken out of the *world*."

STOP! Paul never mentioned anything being taken
out of the <u>world</u>. Paul does not come close to saying any-

thing of the sort. He says, "… taken out of *the way*," not out of *the world*. Not *away*, it is not *taken away*, but *out of the way*. When the time of the Antichrist is come, he will be given his opportunity to do his ungodly blasphemies. When this happens, the restrainer will be moved *out of the way*. What is it then that keeps the Antichrist restrained?

Now I know that there will be those who will say that the *he* found here in verse seven is either the church or the Holy Ghost. However one must understand that the *he* is not taken away but rather the *he* is to be *taken out of the way*. Jesus said in his prayer while in the garden of Gethsemane in John 17:15 "*I pray not that thou shouldest take them out of the world, but that thou shouldest keep them from the evil.*" Jesus Christ my friend has prayed that we will be kept from the evil rather than being *taken out of the world, or from out of the way.* The *he* found here in II Thessalonians 2:7 is none other than Michael the Archangel. Michael is the one restraining the Antichrist. It is Michael the restrainer that will be taken out of the way so that the revelation of the Antichrist might be manifested. Once Michael is taken *out of the way* he will then ascend into the heavens and begin war with Satan to cast him down to the earth. There are several events that will simultaneously take place or occur at the same time. The first event will be the stopping of the daily sacrifice, the

> One must understand that the *he* is not taken away but rather the *he* **is to be** *taken out of the way.*

second event will be the revelation of the Antichrist, and the third sequence of events will be the removal of Michael the Archangel. Michael is the one who restrains until *he* is taken out of the way. When all of these events suddenly and simultaneously take place this will begin the period known as, _The Great Tribulation._ Paul said nothing about anything being taken out of the world. He said plainly that someone *(he)* was to be taken *out of the way.* It is men who have corrupted the Word of God to declare that something is taken out of the world. Paul an apostle of our Lord Jesus Christ said no such thing! *Something is taken out of the way,* not taken away!

We read in Daniel 12:1 *"And at that time Michael shall stand up, the great prince which standeth for the children of thy people: and there shall be a time of trouble such as never was since there was a nation even to that same time."* The word 'standeth' is *amad* #5975 in the Hebrew and it means to rise up mount up or to go up. It will be at this point and time that Michael will rise up or go up into the heavens and start a war with Satan. It will be at this divine appointed time that Jesus Christ our Lord will begin his absolute reign. Victory will start in heaven and work its way down to the earth.

We read in Revelation 12:7-13

> *And there was war in heaven: Michael and his angels fought against the Dragon; and the dragon fought and his angels, and prevailed not; neither was there place found anymore in heaven. And the great dragon was cast out, that old serpent, called the devil, and Satan, which deceiveth the whole world: he was cast out into the earth, and his an-*

*gels were cast out with him. And I heard a loud voice saying in heaven, now is come salvation, and strength, and the kingdom of our God, and the power of his Christ: for the accuser of our brethren is cast down, which accuse them before our God day and night. And they overcame him by the blood of the Lamb, and by the word of their testimony; and they loved not their lives unto the death. Therefore rejoice, ye heavens, and ye that dwell in them. Woe to the inhabitants of the earth and of the sea! for the devil is come down unto you having great wrath, because he knoweth that he has but a short time.*

It is at this appointed time that Satan will forever be vanquished from the throne of God and from his holy presence. Satan will never again have the opportunity to falsely accuse the children of God. Now we read here in Revelation 13:6 *"And he opened his mouth in blasphemy against God, to blaspheme his name, and his tabernacle, and them that dwell in heaven."* We now see that the Antichrist will open his mouth in blasphemy against God. The word *"blasphemy"* is *blasphemia* #988 and in the Greek it means, *"the worst type of slander possible: being desirous to wound one's reputation by evil reports and by evil speaking."* We now have evidence that the Antichrist will blaspheme the name of God, his holy tabernacle in heaven and all of heavens host.

We read in Revelation 13:7 *"And it was given unto him to make war with the saints, and to overcome them: and power was given him over all kindreds, and tongues, and nations."* Many will say that the Saints here are declared to be tribulation saints. However that is conjecture also because the bible does not delineate between tribulation saints or just saints. This will be the church's greatest hour and we must stand having done all to stand in that evil day.

We read in Revelation 13:8 *"And all that dwell upon the earth shall worship him, whose names are not written in the book of life of the Lamb slain from the foundation of the world."* When John declares all that dwell upon the earth shall worship the beast, he is speaking of those whose names are not written in the Lamb's Book of life. At this point and time we are not going to address predestination or election. John declares that the Lamb of God was slain from the foundation of the world or before the world ever existed relative to the creation of Adam and Eve.

Some Jewish scholars and traditions teach that everyone's name is already written in the Lamb's Book of life and if they *do not repent* and accept Jesus Christ as their Lord Savior then their names will be blotted out of the Book of life. The reason that we are able to embrace such a teaching as this is because we read in Exodus 32:32-33 *"Yet now, if thou will forgive their sin--; and if not, blot me, I pray thee, out of thy book which thou hast written. And the Lord said unto Moses, Whosoever hath sinned against me, him will I blot out of my book."* The psalmist also advocated this same teaching found here in Psalm 69:27-28 *"Add iniquity unto their iniquity: and let them not come into thy righteousness. Let them be blotted out of the book of the living, and not be written with the righteous."*

Jesus spoke of a time when a man, the Antichrist,

would come in his own name and he would be received. John 5:43 states, *"I am come in my Father's name, and ye receive Me not; if another shall come in his own name, him ye shall receive."* So it is presently. The world is starving for a One World leader to cure our collective ills. Joblessness, health care, economical and political wars are among them. The world is ready to receive such a man; and yet, contrary to popular teaching about a pre tribulation rapture, the Church is still here. II Thessalonians 2:8-9 states,

> *And then shall that Wicked [One] be revealed, whom the Lord shall consume with the Spirit of His mouth, and shall destroy with the brightness of His coming; even Him, whose coming is after the working of Satan with all power and signs and lying wonders.*

And then shall that the *wicked* (Strong's: Greek #459), the *unholy or lawless* one be revealed, *"whom the Lord shall consume"* (Strong's: Greek #355) or destroy with the Spirit (Strong's: Greek #4151) or "breath" of His mouth, and "shall destroy with *brightness*" (Strong's: Greek #2015), or "the manifestation of His Second Advent in His coming." Notice, the Antichrist will come with all power, signs and lying wonders. This means they have no intrinsic value, but they indicate the Antichrist and his immediate connection with a higher spiritual world, which is Satan himself. No doubt, the Antichrist will be powerful, persuasive and memorable in his acts. The Antichrist is not Satan, but is after the working of Satan. He will be a miracle worker, and in the end, he will challenge all that is good and righteous.

The Antichrist is not Satan, but a man totally under Satan's control. In Revelation 19:20-21, we see the beast and the false prophet are cast into a lake of fire. Then in Revelation 20:1-3, Satan is cast into the bottomless pit. Then 1,000 years later, Satan will be cast into the lake of fire with the Antichrist and false prophet. Revelation 20:10 reads, *"And the devil that deceived them was cast into the lake of fire and brimstone, where the beast and the false prophet are, and shall be tormented day and night for ever and ever."*

II Thessalonians 2:10 reads, *"And with all deceiveableness* (Strong's: Greek #539) or the delusion of unrighteousness (Strong's: Greek #93) or iniquity in "them that perish; because they received not the *love"* (Strong's: Greek #26) or affection "of the *truth"* (Strong's: Greek #225), or the veracity necessary for them to be *saved* (Strong's: Greek #4982), a reference to the future deliverance of believers at the second coming. People will not be saved because they love not the truth. In reading II Thessalonians 2:3, you discover, the "falling away" is not referring to backsliding but to the rejection of Jesus Christ as Lord and Savior. II Thessalonians 2:11 is now more easily understood. *"And for this cause,* the Antichrist's false work and the rejecting of the truth, *God will send them a strong delusion"* (Strong's: Greek #4106), or a point of error that they should then believe (Strong's: Greek #4105) a lie, or that they would have faith to believe or entrust a lie. Then verse 12 reads, *"That they all might be damned"* (Strong's: Greek #2919) or punished *"who believe not the truth"* but had *pleasure* (Strong's: Greek #2106) in unrighteousness, meaning to approbate or think good and therefore, approve of unrighteousness.

So, in this respect, ask yourself, was Yitzhak Rabin's assassination of any relevance? The answer is an emphatic, "Yes." He was a national hero to Israel and was the prominent leader in the Six Day War (June 1967). In that war, the Sinai Desert was captured, as were the West Bank and the Golan Heights. I suppose the reason for the nation's trauma was partly due to Rabin falling from within by an Israeli assassin's bullet. The fact that he was killed by one of his own people will make him even more of a hero. Realize, that just as in II Thessalonians 2:7, Rabin was "taken out of the way." Israel's parliament has 120 seats, and prior to his death, Rabin controlled 61 of them. The land that was won in the Six Day War was rightfully Israel's (see Genesis 15:18-21). Still, Rabin was willing to forfeit the land for the sake of peace—a point which caused anger and resentment against him.

The Middle East conflict is not economical, political, or even geographical. Rather, it is religious. Making peace with Jordan's King Hussein was favorable with most Israelis because they saw him as a respectable man. However, they were not overwhelmed with Yasser Arafat. If you recall, Hussein was at Rabin's funeral, but Arafat was not. His presence would have caused great contention. Most people are not aware that Rabin went further in his negotiations than most had been able to accomplish, including discussions about the control of the Temple Mount and the strategic Golan Heights region in his negotiations with Syria and King Assad.

Rabin knew the elections in Israel were to be held

coinciding with those held in the United States. If the peace process could be moved far enough along, and if he could give enough land away through the signing of documents, then no matter what transpired in the elections, the peace accords could not be revised. Simon Peres, his successor, was more liberal than Rabin. *Peres* means to divide and there was no intent. Pope John Paul ll considered Jerusalem the capitol of Israel, and the capitol of three faiths: Christianity, Islam, and Judaism. My question is global: Who gave the Pope such authority to declare such a thing? The subjugation has begun.

It's here, it's coming—and the Church is still here! Israel is about to be surrounded by Gentiles. The United Nations has called for the internationalizing of Jerusalem. When this happens, all foreign embassies in Israel will be moved from Tel Aviv to Jerusalem. Thus, giving the Anti-Christ his throne from which to rule. No doubt when world pressure rises, these things will come to fruition. Even former U.S. President Bill Clinton declared in his eulogy of Rabin, "As God stood with Moses in the Exodus, even so will America stand with Israel." (Astounding!)

One reason Israel is willing to give up so much land is because someone will make a covenant with Israel (Daniel 9:27). Don't be surprised if soon you see the religious Jews reinstate the animal sacrifices at the Temple Mount.

Rabin's martyrdom will cause these things to be hastened. However, things could have been different had he lived. *"But the end of all things is at hand. Be ye therefore sober and watch unto prayer"* (I Peter 4:7).

To recap, there are three things which presage or foreshadow the coming of the Lord:

1. A sudden acceleration of apostasy from godliness,
2. The removal of some restraining influence,
3. And then a complete unveiling of the incarnation of Evil that will be animated by Satan and will oppose and exalt himself above all that is called God.

*(AP Photo/Wide World Photos/Ron Edmonds)*

Washington (D.C.) September 13, 1993—Israeli Prime Minister Yitzhak Rabin Palestine Liberation Organization Chairman Yasser Arafat and U.S. President Bill Clinton sign a historic peace accord on the South Lawn of the White House.

# CHAPTER 5

# THE
# TRIBULATION

It has, heretofore, been my understanding that the Church will not go through or be present on earth during the tribulation. Thus, I had little knowledge of the wrath of God to be poured out upon the world in the last days of this present age. Having believed we would be gone, it was not necessary for me to study the Scriptures for understanding about God's wrath on a world from which we would be raptured, and a time with which we would not be involved. Jesus said in Matthew 24:21, *"For then shall be great tribulation, such as was not since the beginning of the world to this time, nor ever shall be."* The term *tribulation* (Strong's: Greek #2347) here means to feel pressure, to be afflicted, anguished, burdened or persecuted. Thus, Jesus was simply saying, in that day of tribulation, there will be pressure and anguish upon the world, and it will happen in a way that has never occurred before and will never take place again (see also Luke 21:25-26). Matthew 24:29-31 states,

*Immediately after the tribulation of those days shall the sun be darkened, and the moon shall not give her light, and the stars shall fall from heaven, and the powers of the heavens shall be shaken. And then shall appear the sign of the Son of Man in heaven; and then shall all the tribes of the earth mourn, and they shall see the Son of Man coming in the clouds of heaven with power and great glory. And He shall send His angels with a great sound of a trumpet, and they shall gather together the elect from the four winds, from one end of heaven to the other.*

The term *immediately* (Strong's: Greek #2112) means directly, forthwith, or straightaway. As soon as the tribulation ends, every part of the universe will be darkened and then shall *appear* (Strong's: Greek #1966) or *shine*, the sign of the Son of Man in heaven; and they shall be gathered together, His elect, from the four winds, from one end of heaven to another. The term *together* (Strong's: Greek #1996) means to collect upon the same place. In I Thessalonians 4:17, we read, "... *we will be caught up together with them in the clouds to meet the Lord in the air.*" Notice, the word "together" (Strong's: Greek #260) has a different meaning—at the same time. So, at the same time and the same place we will meet the Lord in the air. I believe the Church will escape *the wrath of God*, just as Israel did in the Exodus, for He will protect His people and His Church.

One writer asked the question in Hebrews 2:3, *"How shall we escape, if we neglect so great salvation; which at first began to be spoken by the Lord and was confirmed unto us by them that heard Him."* If we *neglect* (Strong's: Greek #272), which can mean *to be careless* or *make light* of our *salvation* (Strong's: Greek #4991), our *rescue* from sin or our safety, we will not be delivered and we will receive a just recompense for our unbelief and not trusting God our Savior. Pharaoh was a world dictator, a type of the Antichrist. And, Israel was God's elect (the Church of the Old Testament, the called-out ones). And so it will be in this last hour. As Moses was a deliverer of God's people, so Jesus will deliver us. The one reason I'm confident of God's protection on the Church is due to the fact that Jesus prayed for us 2,000 years ago, as we read in John 17:15, *"I pray not that Thou shouldest take them out of the world, but that Thou shouldest keep them from the evil."*

I know that His prayer will be answered. We read of other prayers He prayed which were answered throughout Scripture. Luke 22:31-32 reads,

> *And the Lord said, 'Simon, Simon, behold, Satan hath desired to have you, that he may sift you as wheat; but, I have prayed for thee, that thy faith fail not; and when thou art converted, strengthen thy brethren.*

The term *prayed* (Strong's: Greek #1189) means "to beg or petition, to make a request." And Jesus did that for Peter, and His prayer was answered. Just as Pharaoh persecuted Israel, the Church needs to get ready for persecution. Look at Exodus 5:6-18:

> *And Pharaoh commanded the same day the task-*
> *masters of the people, and their officers, saying, Ye*
> *shall no more give the people straw to make brick,*
> *as heretofore: let them go and gather straw for*
> *themselves. And the tale of the bricks, which they*
> *did make heretofore, ye shall lay upon them; ye*
> *shall not diminish ought thereof: for they be idle;*
> *therefore they cry, saying, Let us go and sacrifice*
> *to our God. Let there more work be laid upon the*
> *men, that they may labour therein; and let them*
> *not regard vain words. And the taskmasters of*
> *the people went out, and their officers, and they*
> *spake to the people, saying, Thus said Pharaoh,*
> *I will not give you straw. Go ye, get you straw*
> *where you can find it: yet not ought of your work*
> *shall be diminished. So the people were scattered*
> *abroad throughout all the land of Egypt to gath-*
> *er stubble instead of straw. And the taskmasters*
> *hasted them, saying, Fulfill your works, your*
> *daily tasks, as when there was straw.*

As Pharaoh made it difficult for God's people, so it will happen again. The world will rise up in persecution against the Church during this period. Now, having gone back and looked at the wrath of God upon the land of Egypt, we need to make some serious assessments. Look at I Thessalonians 5:3, which reads, *"For when they shall say peace and safety; then sudden destruction cometh upon them, as travail upon a woman with child; and they shall not escape."* Paul is describing destruction that is directed at *them* and *they*, Neither form is a reference to God's people. So it was in the day of Moses. God's people are never the object of wrath. The plagues were directed at

Pharaoh and all of Egypt. Look at Exodus 7:19-25:

*And the Lord spake unto Moses, Say unto Aaron, Take thy rod, and stretch forth thine hand upon the waters of Egypt, upon their streams, upon their rivers, and upon their ponds, and upon all their pools of water, that they may become blood; and that there may be blood throughout all the land of Egypt, both in vessels of wood, and in vessels of stone. And Moses and Aaron did so, as the Lord commanded; and he lifted the rod, and smote the waters that were in the river, in the sight of Pharaoh, and in the sight of his servants, and all the waters that were in the river were turned to blood.*

*And the fish that was in the river died, and the river stank, and the Egyptians could not drink of the water of the river; and there was blood throughout all the land of Egypt. And the magicians of Egypt did so with their enchantments: and Pharaoh's heart was hardened, neither did he hearken unto them; as the Lord said. And Pharaoh turned and went into his house, neither did he set his heart to this also. And all Egyptians digged round about the river for water to drink; for they could not drink of water of the river. And seven days were fulfilled after the Lord had smitten the river.*

Notice the directives in verses 19-21, "... *upon the waters of Egypt, their streams, their rivers, their ponds, the Egyptians could not drink of the water of the river, and there was blood throughout all the land of Egypt.*" All of this is directed at Egypt and not Israel. The next plague was frogs. Look at Exodus 8:1-4:

*And the Lord spake unto Moses, Go unto Pharaoh, and say unto him, Thus saith the Lord, Let My people go, that they may serve Me. And if thou refuse to let them go, behold, I will smite all thy borders with frogs: And the river shall bring forth frogs abundantly, which shall go up and come into thine house of thy servants, and thy people, and in to thine ovens, and into thy kneading troughs: And the frogs shall come up both on thee, and thy people, and upon all thy servants.*

Once again, look at the directives, "... *smite thy borders with frogs ... which shall come into thine house.*" The frogs invaded bedchambers and beds, affected the servants and the people, were found in ovens and kneading troughs. Verse 4 is explicit, "*And the frogs shall come up both on thee and upon <u>thy people</u> and upon <u>thy servants</u>.*" Isn't it insightful, to see how the Egyptians were punished and not one of God's people was affected. In Exodus 8:8, Pharaoh said, "*Entreat the Lord that He may take away the frogs <u>from me</u> and my people.*" Here again, Israel is never talked about in regards to the plagues, it is always Pharaoh and his people.

In the third plague, God smote the land of Egypt with lice. However, when the magicians tried to attempt to duplicate this miracle, they failed and said, "*This is the finger of God*" (see Exodus 8:19). The fourth plague was a swarm of flies. Notice again, God told Moses to direct the plague and God put a division between His people and the people of the world, Egypt. Exodus 8:21 states,

*Else, if thou wilt not let My people go, behold, I will send swarms of flies upon <u>thee</u>, and upon <u>thy servants</u>, and upon <u>thy people</u>, and into <u>thy houses</u>; and the*

*houses of the Egyptians shall be full of swarms of flies,*
*and also the ground whereon they are.*

Look again at the directive, "*I will send swarms of flies upon thee, upon thy people, into thy houses and the houses of the Egyptians shall be full of swarms of flies.*"
Verse 22 states, "*And I will sever in that day the land of Goshen in which My people dwell that no swarms of flies shall be there.*" Verse 23 says, "*And I will put a division between My people and thy people: tomorrow shall this sign be.*" O what power in the word *division* which means—a distinction or even redemption. Yes, there will be a distinction and a great redemption for God's people. God wanted Pharaoh to know His greatness., He could redeem His own elect and keep them, yet destroy others. These were not ordinary flies. They were killer flies. Read Psalm 78:45, "*He sent divers sort of flies among them which devoured them.*"
Recognize the importance of living holy and righteous. Paul said in Ephesians 4:30, "*And grieve not the Holy Spirit.*" Now just as powerfully as God sent this swarm of flies on Pharaoh's people, God removed them. Exodus 8:31 declares, "*And the Lord did according to the word of Moses; and He removed the swarms of flies from Pharaoh, from His servants, and from His people; there remained not one.*" Here again, the removal was from Pharaoh, his servants and from his people. Notice how powerful our God is and also how very particular He is in His dealings. It is amazing He can cause harm to come to one and yet not hurt another. [I will explain more details about this later on in this chapter.]

In the fifth plague, notice God specified what Moses was to say to the Pharaoh. Exodus 9:3-4 reads,

> *Behold, the hand of the Lord is upon thy cattle which is in the field, upon thy horses, upon thy asses, upon thy camels, upon thy oxen, and upon thy sheep: there shall be a very grievous murrain. And the Lord shall sever between the cattle of Israel and the cattle of Egypt: and there shall nothing die of all that is the children's of Israel.*

This was a very grievous plague called *murrain* (Strong's: Hebrew #1698), meaning a destructive pestilence. Once again, the plague was only *"upon thy cattle, upon the horses, upon the asses, upon the camel, upon the oxen and upon the sheep."* Notice God's words in verse 4, *"And the Lord shall sever between the cattle of Israel and the cattle of Egypt: and there shall nothing die of all that is the children's of Israel."* And verse 5 declares, *"And the Lord appointed a set time, saying, 'Tomorrow the Lord shall do this thing in the land,"* God set an appointed time, which He also does in Revelation 9:15, *"And· the four angels were loosed which were prepared for an hour, and a day, and a month, and a year, for to slay the third part of men."* Here we see an appointed time, an hour, a day, a month and a year. God's power and greatness amaze me.

> *And this shall be the plague where with the Lord will smite all the people, that have fought against Jerusalem; their flesh shall consume away in their holes, and their tongue shall consume away in their mouth. And it shall come to pass in that day, that a great tumult from the Lord shall be*

*among them; and they shall lay hold everyone
on the hand of his neighbor.*

*And Judah also shall fight at Jerusalem; and the
wealth of all the heathen round about shall be gathered together, gold and silver, and apparel, in great
abundance. And so shall be the plague of the horse,
of the mule, of the camel, of the ass, and of all the
beasts that shall be in these tents, as this plague.*

*And it shall come to pass, that everyone that is left
of all the nations which came against Jerusalem
shall even go up from year to year to worship the
King, the Lord of hosts, and to keep the feast of tabernacles. And it shall be, that whoso will not come
up of all the families of the earth unto Jerusalem
to worship the King, the Lord of hosts, even upon
them shall be no rain. And if the family of Egypt go
not up, and come not, that have no rain; there shall
be the plague, where with the Lord will smite
the heathen that comes not up to keep the feast
of tabernacles. This shall be the punishment of
Egypt, and the punishment of all the nations
that come not up to keep the feast of tabernacles*
(Zechariah 14:12-19).

During this time, God will smite people on the earth, as
well as animals, with an ugly plague. In verses 18-19, note
that during The Millennium, those who do not worship the
King nor honor the Feast of Tabernacles, to them He will
send no rain, and He specifically identifies Egypt twice.

In Exodus 9:6, the Bible says that all the cattle of Egypt
died; but of the cattle of the children of Israel, not one
died. Nothing of Israel was ever touched by the plagues.

So it will be with God's people during the Tribulation. I must tell you, we will be in the world during The Tribulation. John 17:15 states, *"I pray not that Thou shouldest take them out of the world, but that Thou shouldest keep them from the evil."*

> *And the Lord said unto Moses and unto Aaron, Take to you handfuls of ashes of the furnace, and let Moses sprinkle it toward the heaven in the sight of Pharaoh. And it shall become small dust in all the land of Egypt, and shall be a boil breaking forth with blains upon man, and upon beast, throughout all the land of Egypt. And they took ashes of the furnace, and stood before Pharaoh; and Moses sprinkled it up toward heaven; and it became a boil breaking forth with blains upon man, and upon beast. And the magicians could not stand before Moses because of the boil; for the boil was upon the magicians, and upon all the Egyptians (Exodus 9:8-11).*

Moses was to toss up ashes of the furnace toward heaven in the sight of Pharaoh and it would cause boils to break forth upon man and beast throughout the land of Egypt. The boil spoken of here is a kind of ulcer with a severe inflammation and fever which caused swelling and burning. This plague is somewhat similar to the vial found in Revelation 16:10-11,

> *And the fifth angel poured out his vial upon the seat of the beast; and his kingdom was full of darkness; and they gnawed their tongues for pain, and blasphemed the God of heaven because of their pains and their sores, and repented not for their deeds.*

As never before, I exhort you to follow closely to Christ our Savior for His divine protection. Just as He forbade the four angels in Revelation 7:1-3 to "... *not hurt the earth or the sea*" until He sealed the 144,000, so it will be with us. If we are sealed, we will not be hurt by God's wrath. Ephesians 1:13 states, "*In Whom ye also trusted, after ye heard the word of truth, the gospel of your salvation; in Whom also, after that ye believed, ye were sealed with that Holy Spirit of promise.*" We are sealed with the Holy Spirit of promise and will be kept from the wrath of God.

I Thessalonians 5:9-10 says, "*For God hath not appointed us to wrath, but to obtain salvation by our Lord Jesus Christ. Who died for us, that, whether we wake or sleep, we should live together with Him.*" Look closely at I Thessalonians 1:10. Notice, we are *to wait for His Son* from heaven, whom He raised from the dead, even Jesus which *delivered* (Strong's: Greek #4506) or *rushed to rescue* [in the past tense] us from the *wrath* (Strong's: Greek #1709), the *violent passion or indignation that is to come* (Strong's: Greek #2064) or *appear.* God has predestined to rescue, deliver and protect His Church from the wrath that is to come. Continuing, Exodus 9:13-26 reads:

> *And the Lord said unto Moses, Rise up early in the morning, and stand before Pharaoh, and say unto him, Thus saith the Lord God of the Hebrews, Let My people go, that they may serve Me. For I will at this time send all My plague upon thine heart, and upon thy servants, and upon thy people; that thou mayest know that there is none like Me in all the earth. And in very deed for this cause I have raised thee up, for to shew in thee My power, and that My*

*name may be declared throughout the earth. As yet exaltest thou thyself against My people, that thou wilt not let them go?*

*Behold, tomorrow about this time I will cause it to rain a very grievous hail, such as hath not been in Egypt since the foundation thereof even until now. Send therefore now, and gather thy cattle, and all that thou hast in the field; for upon every man and beast which shall be found in the field, and shall not be brought home, the hail shall come down upon them, and they shall die. He that feared the word of the Lord among the servants of Pharaoh made his servants and his cattle flee into the houses. And he that regarded not the word of the Lord left his servants and his cattle in the field.*

*And the Lord said unto Moses, Stretch forth thine hand toward the heaven, that there may be hail in the land of Egypt, upon man and upon beast, and upon every herb of the field, throughout the land of Egypt. And Moses stretched forth his rod toward heaven; and the Lord sent thunder and hail, and the fire ran along upon the ground, and the Lord rained hail upon the land of Egypt. So there was none like it in all the land of Egypt since it became a nation. And the hail smote throughout the land of Egypt all that was in the field, both man and beast; and the hail smote every herd of the field, and brake every tree of the field. Only in the land of Goshen, where the children of Israel were, was there no hail.*

In Verse 14, we see again God saying, *"I will send all my plagues upon thine heart."* God made Pharaoh's heart hard with these great plagues. This is possibly the worst plague of all, that of a hard and rebellious heart. The same will happen in the end times according to Revelation 9:20-21. Due to the many plagues to come, men will not repent. Here again, God directs the plagues at the world's crowd, along with those who have not obeyed the Gospel. Verse 16: *"For this cause, I have raised thee up, for to shew my power."* The same can be said for the One World Order's system and the Antichrist. Once again, God's power will be made known and His name will be exalted throughout the earth.

In Verse 18, God said, *"I will cause it to rain very grievous hail ...,"* which is similar to Revelation 16:21.

> *And there fell upon men a great hail out of heaven, every stone about the weight of a talent; and men blasphemed God because of the plague of the hail; for the plague thereof was exceeding great.*

The hail in Revelation was awesome, each piece weighing about 114 pounds. For some unknown reason, in Exodus, God allows those in Egypt to escape with their cattle into houses, and those who fled did not suffer greatly. Psalm 130:7 states, *"For with the Lord there is mercy."* No doubt mercy and grace are always shown to every generation; but, only for a time, after which God will cause His word to come to fruition.

> *But as for thee and thy servants, I know that ye will not yet fear the Lord God. And the flax and the barley was smitten; for the barley was in the ear, and the flax was boiled. But the wheat and the rye were not smitten: for they were not grown up,* (Exodus 9:30-32).

We are able to see that God destroyed the flax and barley. No doubt, this would cause famine in the land, and this corresponds to what we find in Revelation 6:6, *"And I heard a voice in the midst of the four beasts say, a measure of wheat for a penny, and three measures of barley for a penny, and see thou hurt not the oil and the wine."* Likewise, in Revelation 6:8, we see Death and Hell use hunger as a means to kill. In Exodus 10:7, Pharaoh's servants asked him, *"How long will this man Moses be a snare to us, knowest thou not yet that Egypt is destroyed?"* What devastation the people saw. Yet, the hardness of Pharaoh's heart kept God's wrath continuing.

Look at the eighth plague found in Exodus 12:12-15,

> *And the Lord said unto Moses, Stretch out thine hand over the land of Egypt for the locusts, that they may come up upon the land of Egypt, and eat every herb of the land, and even all that the hail hath left. And Moses stretched forth his rod over the land of Egypt, and the Lord brought an east wind upon the land all that day, and all that night, and when it was morning, the east wind brought the locusts. And the locusts went up over all the land of Egypt, and rested in all the coasts of Egypt: very grievous were they; before them there were no such locusts as they, neither after them shall be such. For they covered the face of the whole earth, so that the land was darkened; and they did eat every herb of the land, and all the fruit of the trees which the hail had left: and there remained not any green thing in the trees, or in the herbs of the field, through all the land of Egypt.*

In this passage, we see locusts in such great numbers that the whole land was darkened. The locusts ate every herb, every fruit and every leaf left on the trees. We know that the hail and fire had not destroyed all of the vegetation (see Exodus 9:32). We read *"...the wheat and the rye were not smitten, for they were not grown up."* But, with the plague of the locusts, all of the vegetation was destroyed. We find a similar situation in Revelation 9:3-11,

*And there came out of the smoke locusts upon the earth; and unto them was given power, as the scorpions of the earth have power. And it was commanded them that they should not hurt the grass of the earth, neither any green thing, neither any tree; but only those men which have not the seal of God in their foreheads. And to them it was given that they should not kill them, but that they should be tormented five months; and their torment was like the torment of a scorpion, when he striketh a man.*

*And in those days shall men seek death, and shall not find it; and shall desire to die, and death shall flee from them. And the shape of the locusts were like unto horses prepared unto battle; and on their heads were as it wear crowns like gold, and their faces were as the faces of men. And they had hair as the hair of women, and their teeth were as the teeth of lions. And they had breastplates, as it were breastplates of iron, and the sound of their wings was as of the sound of chariots of many horses running to battle. And they had tails like unto scorpions, and their power was to hurt men five months.*

The locusts in Revelation were commanded to torment men five months. One noticeable factor is that the locusts not only torment men for five months, they are also commanded not to harm the grass of the earth, neither any green thing or tree, but only to torment men who do not have the seal of God in their foreheads. Notice that God's commandment is very specific. In Exodus, we saw the locusts being commanded to hurt the earth, and now in Revelation, we find the locusts being commanded not to hurt the earth, but rather to torment men.

Look at Psalm 78:49-50,

> *He cast upon them the fierceness of His anger, wrath, and indignation, and trouble, by sending evil angels among them. He made a way to His anger; He spared not their soul from death, but gave their life over to the pestilence.*

I am convinced that one reason God can destroy certain people, places and elements is because these works are accomplished by evil angels. In Verse 50, David says, *"... He spareth not their souls from death, but gave their life over to the pestilence."* This work was done by evil angels. As I began studying Jude's writings, I discovered an important fact about angels:

> *I will therefore put you in remembrance, though ye once knew this, how that the Lord, having saved the people out of the land of Egypt, afterward destroyed them that believed not. And the angels which kept not their first estate, but left their own habitation, he hath reserved in everlasting chains under darkness unto the judgment of the great day,* (Jude 5, 6).

It is ironic that in Jude's epistle, that he begins to speak in verse 5 about Egypt and how God delivered His people, yet afterward destroyed those who did not believe. Then in verse 6, Jude speaks of angels who left their first estate. These angels could most certainly be the evil angels which David spoke of in Psalm 78:49, *"He hath reserved them in everlasting chains under darkness unto the judgment of the great day."* Now, is it possible, as God wills, that He can loose the chains on these evil angels to work evil against wicked men as He commands? Refer to II Peter 2:4, *"God spared not the angels that sinned, but cast them down to hell, and delivered them in to chains of darkness, to be re-served unto judgment."* Some Bible scholars say that there are some fallen angels loose and some which are chained.

> *And there was war in heaven: Michael and his angels tough t against the dragon; and the dragon fought and his angels, and prevailed not; neither was their place found any more in heaven. And the great dragon was cast out, that old serpent, called the Devil, and Satan, which deceiveth the whole world: he was cast out in to the earth, and his an-gels were cast out with him* (Revelation 12:7-9).

This passage reveals that there are angels loose, fighting and warring. It is obvious that angels can and will make bodily contact with men during the Tribulation. Look at Acts 12:7, which says,

> *And behold, the angel of the Lord came upon him, and a light shined in the prison, and he smote Peter on the side, and raised him up, saying, "Arise up quickly."' And his chains fell off from his hands.*

We see that the angel *smote* (Strong's: Greek #3817) meaning "to strike with less than a violent blow." The angel struck Peter on the side—a clear picture that angels can and do make physical contact.

In Genesis 19:16 we read,

> *And while he lingered, the men [angels] laid hold upon his hand, and upon the hand of his wife, and upon the hand of his two daughters; and the Lord being merciful unto him; and they brought him forth, and set him without the city.*

We see that the angels made physical contact by taking them by the hand. The Church will be here during the tribulation, yet, God will not allow evil angels to touch His people. The good angels of the Lord will encamp around them that fear Him.

Jude spoke of having the evil angels chained until judgment. If so, we can now understand Revelation 7:2-3 which reads,

> *And after these things I saw four angels standing on the four corners of the Earth, holding the four winds of the Earth that the wind should not blow on the earth nor on the sea, nor on any tree, And I saw another angel ascending from the east, having the seal of the living God: and he cried with a loud voice to the four angels, to whom it was given to hurt the earth and the sea.*

No doubt, the judgment day that Jude spoke of is the judgment to be poured out on the earth. In this passage, we see these evil angels are to hurt the earth only after the 144,000 have been sealed. This shows the deity of Christ

Jesus. Matthew 28:18 states, *"And Jesus came and spake unto them saying, All power is given unto me in heaven and in earth."*

> *And what is the exceeding greatness of his power to us-ward who believe, according to the working of his mighty power, which he wrought in Christ, when he raised him from the dead, and set him at his own right hand in heavenly places, far above all principality, and power, and might, and dominion, and every name that is named, not only in this world, but also in that which is to come,* (Ephesians 1:19-21).

He has authority over all power, principality, might, dominion and every name that is named. Look with me at Revelation 9:1-12. These wicked demons of locust have a king over them. Verse 11 says, *"And they had a king over them, which is the angel of the bottomless pit, whose name in the Hebrew tongue is Abaddon,"* but in Greek, the name is *Apollyon*. No matter what their evil names are, Paul declares that Jesus, the Christ of God, has power over every name that is named. So we see just how controlled The Tribulation will be. Certain numbers, as well as certain parts, may only be harmed or destroyed, as God wills, at set times, just as the Antichrist can only rule for forty-two months, no more and no less, as will be directed by God. Look at Revelation 9:13, 14,

> *And the sixth angel sounded, and I heard a voice from the four horns of the golden altar which is before God, saying to the sixth angel which had the trumpet, loose the four angels which are bound in the great river Euphrates.*

John said these angels are bound in the river Euphrates and will be loosed. It is interesting to note how, at a particular time, they will come forth to do their evil work, which will be to destroy the one third part of men. Continuing with verse 15, we read, "*And the four angels were loosed, which were prepared for an hour, and a day, and a month, and a year, for to slay the third part of men.*" Now it appears these four angels that are loosed demonstrate kingship or dominion over two-hundred-thousand horsemen. It is obvious to me that there is military order in Satan's kingdom. Ephesians 6:12 reads, "*For we wrestle not against flesh and blood, but against principalities, against powers, against the rulers of the darkness of this world, against spiritual wickedness in high places.*" What a uniform satanic order in Satan's kingdom; yet, Jesus is Lord above them all! Philippians 2:10 reads, "*That at the name of Jesus every knee should bow, of things in heaven, and things in earth, and things under earth.*" This verse is significant, for it shows that also those things under the earth (such as angels chained under darkness) are subject to our Lord. I understand this may be very heavy to bear and I think it would be important now to give you words of encouragement. Romans 8:34-39 states,

> *Who is He that condemneth? It is Christ that died, yea rather, that is risen again, Who is even at the right hand of God, Who also maketh intercession for us. Who shall separate us from the love of Christ: shall tribulation, or distress, or persecution, or famine, or nakedness, or peril, or sword? As it is written, For thy sake we are killed all the day long: we are accounted as sheep for the slaughter.*

*Nay, in all these things we are more than conquerors through Him that loved us. For I am persuaded, that neither death, nor life, nor angels, nor principalities, nor power, nor things present, nor things to come, nor height, nor depth, nor any other creature, shall be able to separate us from the love God, which is in Christ Jesus our Lord.*

Paul said that Christ makes intercession for us. Look at Hebrews 7:25, *"Wherefore, he is able also to save them to the uttermost that come unto God by him, seeing he ever liveth to make intercession for them."* As a matter of fact, remember, Jesus has prayed already for us all. John 17:15 says, *"I pray that thou shouldest keep them from evil."* His prayer will be answered. In Romans 8:35, Paul asked the question, *"Can tribulation separate us from the love of God or distress, persecution, famine, nakedness, peril or sword?"* Yes, we may be "killed all the day long," spiritually or physically; however, "to live is Christ and to die is gain."

In Romans 8:37, we are declared to be "more than conquerors" and in verse 38, Paul asserts that *"neither death, nor life nor angels"* [no doubt, the evil ones], *"nor principalities, nor powers, things present or things to come shall separate us."* Then he adds, *"...nor height, nor depth, nor any other creature can separate us from God's love."* Is it possible, that the "creature" that Paul spoke of is the locust, the wicked horsemen, in Revelation 9? Only time will tell. But, whatever comes, *"it will not separate me from the love of God,"* and that's what counts the most.

I want us to go back to the last two plagues and examine them again. Look at Exodus 10:21-23:

*And the Lord said unto Moses, Stretch out thine hand toward heaven, that there may be darkness which may be felt. And Moses stretched forth his hand toward heaven, and there was a thick darkness in all the land of Egypt for three days; they saw not one another, neither rose any from his place for three days; but all the children of Israel had light in their dwellings.*

This was a powerful darkness, without a doubt. So dark, it could be felt; and so dark that fabricated light of any matter could not penetrate it. Again, notice that the darkness was all over Egypt and that the Egyptians could not see one another, neither could they go anywhere for three days. In Jude. 13, we read, "... *the ungodly have a particular darkness awaiting them, to whom is reserved the blackness of darkness forever.*"

But isn't it wonderful to see that all the children of Israel had light in their dwellings. That is the promise of God in John 8:12, "*Then spake Jesus again unto them, saying, 'I am the light of the world: He that followeth me shall not walk in darkness, but shall have the light of life.'*" No matter how dark it may become, we have a light in Christ. John 1:5 notes, "*And the light shineth in the darkness, and the darkness comprehended it not.*" It is very important to remember the words of Paul. I Thessalonians 5:4 reads, "*Ye are the children of light, and the children of day; we are not of the night, nor of darkness.*" We are to be so sober and vigilant in Christ when the trouble hits. We are in the light of Christ and not in darkness.

In closing, let's look at the last plague in Exodus 11:1-10,

*And the Lord said unto Moses, yet will I bring one plague upon Pharaoh, and upon Egypt; afterward he will let you go hence: when he shall let you go, he shall surely thrust you out hence altogether. Speak now in the ears of the people, and let every man borrow of his neighbor, and every woman of her neighbor, jewels of silver, and jewels of gold.*

*And the Lord gave the people favour in the sight of the Egyptians. Moreover, the man Moses was very great in the land of Egypt, in the sight of Pharaoh's servants, and in the sight of the people. And Moses said, thus saith the Lord, about midnight will I go out into the midst of Egypt; and all the firstborn in the land of Egypt shall die, from the firstborn of Pharaoh that sitteth upon his throne, even unto the firstborn of the maidservant that is behind the mill; and all the firstborn of the beasts.*

Right this moment, God is raising up unknown men, who like Moses, will proclaim what is coming. Spurn not their words.

*And there shall be a great cry throughout all the land of Egypt, such as there was none like it, nor shall be like it any more. But against any of the children of Israel shall not a dog move his tongue, against man or beast: that ye may know how that the Lord doth put a difference between the Egyptians and Israel. And all these thy servants shall come down unto me, and all the people that follow thee; and after that I will go out. And he went out from Pharaoh in a great anger. And the Lord said*

*unto Moses, Pharaoh shall not hearken unto you;*
*that My wonders may be multiplied in the land of*
*Egypt. And Moses and Aaron did all these wonders*
*before Pharaoh; and the Lord hardened Pharaoh's*
*heart, so that he would not let the children of Israel*
*go out of his land.*

God was going to bring just one more plague. However, he gave Israel favor with the Egyptians with jewels of gold and silver. It is important to notice the man of God, Moses was a very great man in the land of Egypt; both in the sight of Pharaoh's servants and in the sight of the common people of Egypt. God has raised up His men for such an hour as this, to warn God's people. In the name of the Son of the Living God, take heed to the men and prophets of God in this hour. Right this moment, God is raising up unknown men, who, just like Moses, will proclaim what is coming. Spurn not their words; take heed. Mark 13:23, *"But take ye heed: behold, I have foretold you all things."*

I believe, as Stephen spoke of the church in the wilderness in Acts 7:38, the Israelites are symbolic of the Church. Egypt represents the world and Pharaoh represents an oppressive dictator, the one world leader. Consider me a fool, but Jesus has forewarned us all through the Word of God. In Exodus 11:7, God prophesied that not even a dog of the Israelites would howl during the last plague. For God's greatest secret of all was with his children. In verse 8, God prophetically said to Moses, they will be "urgent" upon you and all of Israel, so they were to make haste and get out of Egypt, for they will declare themselves to be "dead men"(Exodus 12:33). We see in Exodus 11:8, Moses went out from Pharaoh's presence angry, due to the fact he was rebellious and stubborn, and had lied to him over and over. Yet Jehovah knew this last plague would be the one to release Israel. The secret that I spoke of was the blood.

> For the Lord will pass through to smite the Egyptians; and when He seeth the blood upon the lintel, and on the side posts, the Lord will pass over the door, and will not suffer the destroyer to come in unto your houses to smite you, (Exodus 12:23).

I find it very significant that the Lord Himself did a personal inspection of every Israelite home. When He did, it was required that He see the blood. And, so it will be in the Tribulation. Revelation 12:11 says, *"And they overcame him by the blood of the Lamb, and by the word of their testimony, and they loved not their lives unto the death."* We are assured that we will overcome if we are covered by the blood.

I am aware that this is totally in opposition to what a "pre-tribulation rapturist" is supposed to believe, but, as I said earlier, there is never a difference between a "rapture'" and a "Second Advent." I encourage you to go back to the basics of God's Word and take a second look at the second coming.

> This second epistle, beloved, I now write unto you; in both which I stir up your pure minds by way of remembrance; that ye may be mindful of the words which were spoken before by the holy prophets, and of the commandment of us the apostles of the Lord and Saviour: knowing first, that there shall come in the last days scoffers, walking after their own lusts, and saying, Where is the promise of His coming? for since the fathers fell asleep, all things continue

*as they were from the beginning of the creation.*

*For this they willingly are ignorant of, that by the word of God the heavens were of old, and the earth standing out of the water and in the water; whereby the world that then was, being overflowed with water, perished; but the heavens and the earth, which are now, by the same word are kept in store, reserved unto fire against the day of judgment and perdition of ungodly men. But, beloved, be not ignorant of this one thing, that one day is with the Lord as a thousand years, and a thousand years as one day. The Lord is not slack concerning His promise, as some men count slackness; but is longsuffering to us-ward, not willing that any should perish, but that all should come to repentance.*

*But the day of the Lord will come as a thief in the night; in which the heavens shall pass away with a great noise, and the elements shall melt with fervent heat, and the earth also and the works that are therein shall be burned up.*

*Seeing then that all these things shall be dissolved, what manner of persons ought ye to be in all holy conversation and godliness, Looking for and hasting unto the coming of the day of God, wherein the heavens being on fire shall be dissolved, and the elements shall melt with fervent heat?*

*Nevertheless we, according to His promise, look for a new heavens and a new earth', wherein dwelleth righteousness. Wherefore, beloved, seeing that ye look for such things, be diligent that ye may be found in Him in peace, without spot, and blameless, (*II Peter 3:1-14*).*

In looking at this last passage of scripture, we see a very solemn warning. The heavens will pass away with great noise and the elements shall melt with fervent heat. Peter says, *"...seeing and knowing all these things shall be dissolved (or come to pass) what manner of persons ought we to be in all holy conversation and godliness."* If, as pre-tribulation rapture teachings state, the Church is gone, then why do we receive such a solemn warning to live blameless?

- Verse 12: *"... looking for and hasting unto the coming of the day of God..."* Here again, Peter is telling the people 'to look for the coming of the Lord.' And again, there is no difference between a rapture and the Second Advent.

- Verse 14: *"Wherefore, beloved seeing that ye look for such things, be diligent, that ye may be found in Him in peace, without spot, and blameless."* Only in Christ do we find refuge. If we are looking for such things, and therefore, as Peter implied, here when these things come to pass, we must come closer to his presence.

> There is no distinction made between a rapture and the Second Advent. They are both the same.

God will give the needed glory to the Church. Zechariah 2:5 states, *"For I, saith the Lord, will be unto her a wall of fire round about, and will be the glory in the midst of her."* We, the Church, have forgotten that it is *"a fearful thing to fall into the hands of a living God."* My heart is filled with great sorrow because today's Church is full of tepidity and few are preaching what is really coming. God have mercy on us all. There will only be a rapture at the Second Advent.

> *Come, My people, enter thou into thy chambers, and shut thy doors about thee: hide thyself as it were for a little moment, until the indignation be overpast. For, behold, the Lord cometh out of His place to punish the inhabitants of the earth for their iniquity; the earth shall disclose her blood, and shall nor more cover her slain,* (Isaiah 26:20-21).

As we read in James 5:7-8,

> *Be patient therefore, brethren, unto the coming of the Lord. Behold, the husbandman waiteth for the precious fruit of the earth, and hath long patience for it, until he receive the early and latter rain. Be ye also patient; stablish your hearts: for the coming of the Lord draweth nigh.*

We are told to be patient until *"the coming of the Lord."* Here again, there is no distinction made between a rapture and the Second Advent. They are both the same. Patience will certainly be needed during this coming hour. Luke 21:19, *"Jesus said, In your patience possess ye your souls."* Now is the time to get your house in order. First, take care of the spiritual. Get out of debt. Next, take all necessary measures to get godly counsel. Godly men may not tell you what you *want* to hear, but they will be instrumentally used by God to get you directed into the Holy Place. Notice, I said "Holy Place." If you are not living a holy life, all the physical preparation you do will not help you. Jesus is your refuge. Proverbs 27:12 declares, *"A prudent man forseeth the evil and hideth himself, but the simple pass on and are punished."*

As I said earlier, this experience was by "revelation." A short time ago, I was totally convinced of a pre-tribulation rapture. Today, by the grace of God and by the revelation of His Spirit, I am convinced that the Church will be present on earth during the tribulation. Please prayerfully seek God's counsel and direction. Take my word. You're going to need it.

# CHAPTER 6

# THE
# RESURRECTION
# OF THE DEAD

Often times, when addressing the rapture or the Second Advent of Jesus Christ, we fail to understand that the Second Advent of Christ also involves the resurrection of the saints, those who have died in Christ Jesus. In my 35 years of Bible study, I have never seen one prophecy teacher address the resurrection of the saints and couple it with the rapture of the church. The reason, of course, is the contradiction that it poses. It would be too costly to their logic; the two views oppose one another with respect to a pre-tribulation position and the coming of Christ our Lord. The anomaly in separating the two entities makes them contradictory: though, they are the same events and must be coupled. In spite of erroneous teachings, we must realize, that the resurrection is very much a part of the rapture of the sainted dead and of the living righteous. Let us be perfectly clear—there are not *several* resurrections in the *first* resurrection. Jesus Himself only taught *two resurrections!*

The word *resurrection* is never found in the Old Testament. However, that does not negate the fact that the doctrine of the resurrection *is not* taught in the Old Testament. The truth is, the doctrine of the resurrection is one of the greatest teachings found in Old Testament scriptures. It is the doctrine of the resurrection that gave the Old Testament saints their blessed hope of eternal life. Without this understanding and belief, they, too, would have been hopeless concerning their spiritual state after their death. They knew all too well that they had to wait for their Redeemer and Savior to come, for the promise of the resurrection to be fulfilled and brought to fruition. One of the first mentions of the resurrection is in Job 19:25-27,

> *For I know that my redeemer liveth, and that he shall stand at the latter-day upon the earth: and though after my skin worms destroy this body, yet it my flesh shall I see God: whom I shall see for myself, and mine eye shall behold, and not another; though my reins (mind) be consumed with in me.*

In this passage, Job absolutely without doubt refutes a pre-tribulation rapture. The reason we know that Job is refuting a pre-tribulation rapture is because he declared, that "my <u>Redeemer</u>," speaking of the Lord Jesus Christ, shall stand at the latter-day upon the earth, escorting him at his resurrection. Job clearly states, that once Christ Jesus stands upon the earth in the latter or last day, that he shall behold Christ with his own eyes. One Hebrew translation reads this way, *"After I shall awake, though this body is destroyed, yet out of my flesh shall I see God."*

The following passage also correlates with Job's words, *"Beloved, now are we the sons of God, and it doth not yet appear what we shall be: but we know that, when he shall appear, we shall be like him; for we shall see him as he is,"* (I John 3:2). Job does not teach or advocate a secret rapture of the church, nor a secret coming of Christ to resurrect the sainted dead, then returning back to heaven. Rather, Job declares one literal second coming of Jesus Christ, and that *"He (Jesus Christ) will stand upon the earth at the last day."* Job makes that plain and simple. He equates Christ's second coming to his own resurrection as being the same event and as occurring at the same time.

Jesus also said that he would "raise" those that "the Father drew to Himself in the last day." Notice John 6:44, *"No man can come to me, except the Father which hath sent me draw him: and I will raise him up at the last day."* In the New Testament, Martha understood, just as Job, that Christ Jesus would raise the dead at the last day at His second coming. We read in John 11:24, *"Martha saith unto him, I know that he shall rise again in the resurrection at the last day."*

The next passage that we want to address in the Old Testament is Isaiah 26:19,

> *Thy dead men shall live, together with my dead body shall they arise. Awake and sing, ye that dwell in dust: for thy dew is as the dew of herbs, and the earth shall cast out the dead.*

In this passage, Isaiah declares that the "dead men" of Israel that were in Christ Jesus would be resurrected and that Isaiah himself would rise together with them. When Isaiah declared, "*awake and sing*," he is alluding to the trump of God that will awaken those that are dead in Christ, referring to those that dwell in the dust of the earth. Then Isaiah said, "*for as is the dew*"—meaning that dew revives and refreshes the earth. The saints of God will be revived at Christ's second coming and arise from their graves.

We read in Daniel 12:2, "*And many of them that sleep in the dust of the earth shall awake, some to everlasting life, and some to shame and everlasting contempt.*" Isaiah and Daniel both allude to the redeemed that are in the dust of the earth who shall arise and be awakened in *the first resurrection.* Their dead bodies are presently asleep in the dust of the earth. Their soul and spirit are now with the Lord following His resurrection. Just like all the sainted dead, they are awaiting the resurrection of their dead bodies to be reunited with their soul and spirit. I want to be very pointed concerning this passage in Daniel and state without any reservation, that there are only two resurrections: the first resurrection is for those who are resurrected unto everlasting life; and the second resurrection, is for those who are resurrected unto eternal shame and everlasting contempt. This particular scripture passage clearly teaches the doctrine of a first and a second resurrection.

However, it does not disclose the thousand-year millennial reign of Christ between the two resurrections. This passage does not even come close to substantiating a pre-tribulation rapture doctrine, not whatsoever. Needless to say, throughout the Scriptures, both the Old and New Testaments, we have seen many temporary physical resurrections. Elijah had a temporal resurrection in his ministry which can be found in I Kings 17:21-22,

> *And he stretched himself upon the child three times, and cried unto the Lord, and said, O Lord my God, I pray thee, let this child's soul some into him again. And the Lord heard the voice of Elijah; and the soul of the child came into him again, and he revived.*

There is another Old Testament resurrection in the ministry of Elisha in II Kings 4:34,

> *And he went up, and lay upon the child, and put his mouth upon his mouth, and his eyes upon his eyes, and his hands upon his hands: and he stretched himself upon the child; and the flesh of the child waxed warm.*

There is yet another Old Testament resurrection in II Kings 13:20-21,

> *And Elisha died, and they buried him. And the bands of the Moabites invaded the land at the coming in of the year. And it came to pass, as they were burying a man, that, behold, they spied a band of men; and they cast the man into the sepulcher of Elisha: and when the man was let down, and touched the bones of Elisha, he revived, and stood up on his feet.*

And last but not least, there is the resurrection of Jonah. Some teach that Jonah never actually died, but Jesus Christ refutes that fallacy in Matthew 12:40, *"For as Jonas was three days and three nights in the whale's belly; so shall the Son of man be three days and three nights in the heart of the earth."* If Jonah was not truly dead and then resurrected, Jesus would have misled us concerning His own resurrection.

In the New Testament, we find the resurrection of the daughter of Jairus in Mark 5:35-43. We also see the resurrection of Lazarus in John 11:38-45. Then there were those that arose at Christ's resurrection found in Matthew 27:52-53. And there is in Acts 20:9-12, the raising of Eutychus from the dead in the ministry of Paul. Though all these people were resurrected, they still died again by a natural death. If they remained in Christ, they will be resurrected again in the first resurrection.

Let me say, that those resurrected in Matthew 27:52-53, were in the procession of captives that Jesus led with him. Paul, the apostle, spoke of this in Ephesians 4:8, *"Wherefore he saith, 'When he ascended up on high, he led captivity captive, and gave gifts unto men.'"* These saints were alive in soul and spirit, but could not be set free from paradise until Christ had conquered death and hell and He Himself had been raised from the dead. Paul declared in Hebrews 2:14, *"Forasmuch then as the children are partakers of flesh and blood, he also Himself likewise took part of the same; that through death He might destroy him that had the power of death, that is, the devil."* Christ also declared in Revelation 1:18, *"I am He that liveth, and was dead, and, behold, I am alive for evermore, Amen; and have the keys of hell and of death."* When Jesus Christ was resurrected, the captive souls and spirits in paradise were liberated and allowed to go to heaven.

There will be two resurrections in the life of the believer, the child of God. The first one is a spiritual resurrection. The spirit of man is quickened to life from a condition of death due to his trespasses and sins. This is the new birth. Thus Paul declared in II Corinthians 5:17, *"Therefore if any man be in Christ, he is a new creature: old things are passed away; behold, all things are become new."* We must fully understand, that if one does not experience the first resurrection, the spiritual resurrection, newness of life in Christ, he will never experience the material or physical resurrection that is promised at the second coming of Christ. The physical resurrection will be for those saints that have died in Christ. They will be raised by the quickening power of the Holy Ghost at Christ's second coming.

Might I declare, it is the spirit of holiness that will be the very power that will raise those who have died in Christ. That passage is in Romans 1:3-4,

> *Concerning His son Jesus Christ our Lord, which was made of the seed of David according to the flesh; and declared to be the son of God with power, according to the spirit of holiness, by the resurrection from the dead.*

One must possess the spirit of Christ to be resurrected. Paul declared in Romans. 8:9, "Now if any man have not the Spirit of Christ he is none of his." Paul also declared in Romans 8:11, *"But if the spirit of him that raised Jesus from the dead dwell in you, he that raised Christ from the dead shall also quicken your mortal bodies by his spirit that dwelleth in you."*

Jesus Christ was the first to be *eternally* resurrected and now he is seated at the right hand of the throne of

God. Jesus Himself only taught two resurrections during His earthly ministry. Many try to teach, so as to maintain the pre-tribulation doctrine, that there are multiple resurrections in the first resurrection. That is cynical and nonsense. That is like saying, there are three "first" bases on a baseball diamond. Jesus made the resurrections clear. Read John 5:28-29,

> *Marvel not at this: for the hour is coming, in the which all that are in the graves shall hear his voice, and shall come forth; they that have done good under the resurrection of life; and they that have done evil, unto the resurrection of damnation.*

One must understand, all that actually dies in death is the body when one's earthly life has terminated. Death is an entity. Paul declared in I Corinthians 15:55-56, "*O death, where is thy sting? O grave where is thy victory? The sting of death is sin; and the strength of sin is the law.*" When wicked and sinful men die without Christ, there is a sting in their soul and spirit that mortal men could never fathom! One Greek translation reads that the sting is a *goad* or a *poison*. How poisonous sin must be, when left unchecked by the blood of the Lamb! We know that death is an entity, for it rides the pale horse in Revelation 6:8, "*And I looked, and behold a pale horse: and his name that sat on him was Death, and Hell followed with him.*" We are also able to see the eternal demise of both death and hell when they are cast into the lake of fire. Note Revelation 20:13-15,

> *And the sea gave up the dead which were in it; and death and hell delivered up the dead which were in*

*them: and they were judged every man according to their works. And death and hell were cast into the lake of fire. This is the second death.*

This event, known as the second death, occurs after the thousand-year millennial reign of Christ our Lord. Let it be understood, there is no such thing as "soul sleep." The *body* of man is asleep while in the earth and the body has no consciousness while in the earth; however, the soul and spirit are alive and well, having complete awareness and having all five senses. Now that Christ has been resurrected and sits at the right hand of the Father, both the soul and spirit of true believers go to be with the Lord at death; that is, providing they were born again, having experienced the spiritual resurrection from their sins in Christ Jesus. Paul also taught that doctrine in II Corinthians 5:6-9,

> *Therefore we are always confident, knowing that, whilst we are at home in the body, we are absent from the Lord: (For we walk by faith, not by sight). We are confident, I say, and willing rather to be absent from the body, and to be present with the Lord. Wherefore we labor, that, whether present or absent, we may be accepted of him.*

Paul also taught that there were only two resurrections: Acts 24:15, *"And have hope toward God, which they themselves also allow, that there shall be a resurrection of the dead, both of the <u>just and the unjust</u>."* Let it be fully understood that the redeemed go to be with the Lord at their death and the lost or wicked go directly to hell. Psalms 9:17 declares, *"The wicked shall* *be turned into hell, and all the nations that forget God."*

There is no biblical doctrine known as purgatory. Once a soul goes out into eternity, there are no second chances. Life itself is a probationary period. If one does not make it right on this side of eternity, there will be no opportunity to make it right on the other side. Remember the words of Jesus in John.5:28, *"All that are in the graves shall hear His voice."* The dead in Christ will hear His voice at the first resurrection and the wicked dead that died without Christ, will hear His voice at the second resurrection. The same voice that raised the righteous dead from their graves will also call forth the wicked dead from their graves at the second resurrection, which will occur a thousand years later. Every soul of mankind, along with their spirit, will be brought back from heaven or hell and reunited with their bodies at their specified resurrection. The dead in Christ will be reunited with their bodies at the first resurrection. The wicked dead and those that are eternally lost will be reunited with their dead bodies at the second resurrection.

Sometime ago, the Lord showed me that those who go to hell will spend all eternity with whatever sickness or disease they died with. Think of that profundity! The wicked or lost souls do not get a new body like the believer: the lost will retain that old diseased and corrupt body. Whatever anomaly or physical aberrance, whatever their condition at death, they will keep for all eternity. That to me, in and of itself, is absolute horror. The Lord also showed me that the lost are eternally naked. They will never wear a garment of righteousness, or for that matter a garment of any kind, in order to cover their nakedness. Thus, they will forever feel vulnerable and insecure throughout all of eternity. Just as people were stripped and made to feel vulnerable in the concentration camps of World War II, so they will be in hell and far worse, since there is no escaping hell.

Let us now continue our exploration of Revelation 20:4-6,

*And I saw thrones, and they sat upon them, and judgment was given unto them: and I saw the souls of them that were beheaded the for the witness of Jesus, and for the word of God, and of which had not worshiped the beast, neither his image, neither had received his mark upon therefore heads, or in their hands; and they lived and reigned with Christ of files and years. But the rest of the dead lift not again until the thousand years were finished. This is the first resurrection. Blessed and holy is he that hath part in the first resurrection: on such the second death hath no power, but they shall be priest of God and of Christ, and shall reign with him a thousand years.*

> The saints of God will sit upon the thrones and will rule with Christ as kings and priests for one thousand years.

Notice that verse four describes thrones and those that sit upon the thrones will be the saints of God, and they will rule with Christ as kings and priests for one thousand years. We read in Revelation 1:6, *"And hath made us kings and priests unto God and his father; to him be glory and dominion forever and ever. Amen."* I want you to understand, according to Revelation 20:4-6, those who were "beheaded for the witness of Jesus Christ," and those that were beheaded "for the Word of God," and those that did not "worship" the beast, "neither his image, neither had received his mark" upon their foreheads or in their hands, these all lived and reigned with Christ a thousand years. Notice, that all of them were in *the first resurrection*. Once again, to teach multiple resurrections, one would fall into false doctrine and false teaching.

Remember, Christ Himself said that there are only two resurrections—one for those that have done good and the other for those that have done evil. The first resurrection is better known as "the resurrection of life" and the second resurrection is known as "the resurrection of damnation." The resurrection of the righteous is the first resurrection. Thus we are told, "... *blessed and holy is he that will have part in the first resurrection wherein the second death hath no power over them.*"

The resurrection of the wicked is a thousand years later and their resurrection is for the purpose of sentencing them to eternal punishment, damnation and separation from God Almighty. Those wicked people will be resurrected for the purpose of standing before God at the Great White Throne Judgment. We read in Revelation 20:11-15,

> *And I saw great white throne, and him that sat on it, from whose face the earth and the heaven fled away; and there was found no place for them. And I saw the dead, small and great, stand before God; and the books were opened: and another book was opened, which is the book of life: and the dead were judged out of those things which were written in*

*the books, according to their works. And the sea
gave up the dead which were in it; and death and
hell delivered up the dead which were in them:
and they were judged every man according to their
works. And death and hell were cast into the lake of
fire. This is the second death. And whosoever was
not found written in the book of life was cast in to
the lake of fire.*

I am well aware that many of my detractors will try and
use the two witnesses found in Revelation 11, purporting
and attempting to prove multiple resurrections. But let us
look closely at the two witnesses and their resurrection
along with the timing of their resurrection. First of all, let
us establish the fact that there are seven trumpets to be
sounded in the book of Revelation. What happens at the
resurrection of the dead? Paul describes the protocol in I
Thessalonians 4:13-18,

*But I would not have you to be ignorant (through
lack of information), brethren, concerning them
which are asleep, that ye sorrow not, even as others which have no hope. For if we believe that Jesus
died and rose again, even so them also which sleep
in Jesus will God bring with him. For this we say
unto you by the word of the Lord, that we which
are alive and remain unto the coming of the Lord
shall not prevent them which are asleep.*

*For the Lord himself shall descend from heaven
with a shout, with the voice of the archangel, and
with the trump of God: and the dead in Christ shall
rise first: then we which are alive and remain shall
be caught up together with them in the clouds, to*

*meet the Lord in the air: and so shall we ever be*
*with the Lord. Wherefore comfort one another*
*with these words.*

All the dead in Christ shall be awakened by this trumpet. We know in the book of Revelation there are seven trumpets. Now notice Paul's words in I Corinthians 15:51-52,

*Behold, I shew you a mystery; we shall not all sleep,*
*but we shall all be changed, in a moment, in the*
*twinkling of an eye, at the last trumpet: for the*
*trumpet shall sound, and the dead shall be raised*
*incorruptible, and we shall be changed.*

I want to emphasize the phrase—*at the last trumpet.* You may ask why? Because it is at the last trump or at the sounding of the seventh trumpet, that we, the saints of God, along with the two witnesses, shall be raised as noted here in Revelation 11:15, "*And the seventh angel sounded; and there were great voices in heaven, saying, The kingdoms of this world are become the kingdoms of our Lord, and of his Christ; and he shall reign forever and ever.*" These two witnesses will be resurrected and caught up into heaven with the same voice of God and with the "last trumpet" to which Paul alluded to in I Thessalonians 4:13-18. Notice Revelation 11:15-18,

*And the seventh Angel sounded; and there were*
*great voices in heaven, saying, the kingdoms of this*
*world are become the kingdoms of our Lord, and of*
*his Christ; and he shall reign forever and ever.*

*And the four and twenty elders, which sat before God on their seats, fell upon their faces, and worshipped God, saying, we give thee thanks, O Lord God Almighty, which art, and wast, and art to come; because thou hast taken to thee thy great power, and hast reigned.*

*And the nations were angry, and the wrath is come, and the time of the dead, that they should be judged, and that thou shouldest give reward unto thy servants the prophets, and to the saints, and them that fear thy name, small and great; and shouldest destroy them which destroy the earth.*

Now let us go back and do a very short exegesis on this passage of scripture. The seventh angel has sounded the last and final trumpet. There were great voices in heaven, declaring that the kingdoms of this world have now become the kingdoms of our Lord. Now look closely at *v. 18:* "*... the nations were angry and now the time of God's wrath is come,*" meaning, God is about to pour out the seven vials or bowls of judgment upon the earth. *But notice the wrath of God is not yet come: why?* Because, we read in I Thessalonians 5:9-11,

*For God hath not appointed us to wrath, but to obtain salvation by our Lord Jesus Christ, who died for us, that whether we wake or sleep we should live together with him. Wherefore comfort yourselves together and edify one another, even as also ye do*

We also read in Romans 5:9, "*Much more then, being now justified by his blood, we shall be saved from wrath through him.*" Let it be completely understood, although we will suffer great tribulation, we are not appointed unto the wrath of God as is clearly seen in the scriptures. We read in Acts 14:22, "*And that we must through much tribulation enter into the kingdom of God.*"

Again, looking at Revelation 11:18, we can now see, "*… the time of the righteous dead that they should be judged, and the giving of rewards unto His servants the prophets, to the saints, and to them that fear thy name, both small and great.*"

Let us now look closely at what happens here. The giving of these rewards can only be to the righteous; for those receiving these rewards are in the first resurrection. Remember, the second resurrection is for the wicked dead and the damned, and that resurrection will not be for yet another thousand years. Furthermore, if the church has already been removed from the earth, why is Christ giving rewards to prophets, since prophets are one of the fivefold ministry gifts to the church? Does Christ intend to call prophets again during the great tribulation? We know from the scriptures, that the resurrection is a mystery. We read in I Corinthians 15:51-52,

> *Behold I show you a mystery; we shall not all sleep, but we shall all be changed. In a moment, in the twinkling of an eye, at the last trump: for the trumpet shall sound, and the dead shall be raised incorruptible, and we shall be changed.*

This mystery will be fulfilled at the sounding of the seventh and last trump. Look closely at Revelation 10:7, "*But in the days of the voice of the seventh angel, when he shall begin to sound, <u>the mystery of God should be finished, as he hath declared to his servants</u>*

*the prophets.*" What a day that will be when this mystery is completed and fulfilled in behalf of the sainted dead. Every saint of God will be raised from the dead and they will receive a new body; thus, dust shall sing again and this mystery shall be fulfilled and completed!

We trust somehow, that your eyes have been opened to these profound biblical truths. My writings are not for contention, but rather for clarity. Some people get dismayed with me when I claim Galatians 1:11-12 as an experience in my own life, but I do so humbly and sincerely, *"I certify ... brethren, that the gospel which was preached of me is not after man. For I neither received of man, neither was I taught it, but by the revelation of Jesus Christ."*

What I am sharing with you no man has ever taught me, neither did I arrive at this understanding by someone else's books or teachings. All my life I was taught the pre-tribulation doctrine and that was why I taught and preached that doctrine as well. At one point in my life, I simply got so hungry for God, that I spent forty days fasting and seeking His face. And Wow! This revelation came through loud and clear. Needless to say, I have suffered great pain and rejection, along with being called a lot of ugly things for what I now preach and advocate. However, that element of suffering is part of God's calling and election. We will all suffer the loss of many things so that we might know Christ and know Him in the power of His resurrection. This is a true revelation from Jesus Christ, and it is to the body of Christ, our Lord Jesus. May you be blessed by His word as you continue your pilgrimage.

There shall be a resurrection for both the sainted dead

and the wicked dead! *"Blessed and holy is he that hath part in the first resurrection!"*

In Christ,

Evangelist David W. Lankford

# QUESTIONS TO PONDER

1. Where are scripture references for a seven year tribulation? (excluding Daniel 9:27)

2. What is the length of the reign of the Antichrist?

3. Where are the scripture references of the length of the marriage supper of the Lamb?

4. Where are the scripture references to the marriage supper of the Lamb being in heaven?

5. Where are the scripture references to our reigning in heaven with Christ during The Tribulation?

6. How do we know when Daniel's last week has begun?

7. Since Jesus said He would come again, did He mean in two stages? (Hebrews 9:28)

# REFERENCES

*Dake's Annotated Reference Bible.* Finis Jennings Dake, 1961, 1963.

The *Hebrew-Strong's: Greek Key Study Bible,* King James Version: Zodhiates, original and complete system of Bible study. Spiros Sodhiates, Th.D. AMG Publishers, Chattanooga, TN. Ninth Edition, August 1990.

*The Holy Bible,* King James Version. Thomas Nelson Publishers, Nashville, TN. 1976.